Letters to Merline
(1919–1922)

EUROPEAN SOURCES

Russell Epprecht, Series Editor

American Journals
Albert Camus

Diary of an Unknown
Jean Cocteau

Letters to Gala
Paul Eluard

Letters to Merline
Rainer Maria Rilke

Letters

TO

Merline

(1919–1922)

Rainer Maria Rilke

TRANSLATED BY

Jesse Browner

PARAGON HOUSE

New York

First American edition, 1989

Published in the United States by

Paragon House Publishers
90 Fifth Avenue
New York, NY 10011

Originally published in French under the title *Lettres Françaises a Merline, 1919–1922.* Copyright © 1950 by Éditions du Seuil.

Manufactured in the United States of America

Library of Congress Cataloging-in-Publication Data

Rilke, Rainer Maria, 1875–1926.
  [Lettres françaises à Merline, 1919–1922.   English]
  Letters to Merline, 1919–1922 / Rainer Maria Rilke; translated by Jesse Browner.—1st American ed.
     p.   cm.
  Translation of: Lettres françaises à Merline, 1919–1922.
  ISBN 1-55778-115-X
  1. Rilke, Rainer Maria, 1875–1926—Correspondence.   2. Merline—Correspondence.   3. Authors, German—20th century—Correspondence.
I. Merline.   II. Title.
PT2635.I65M4713   1988
831'.912—dc19
[B]   88-1716
                                                             CIP

Introduction

In 1903, sixteen years before the beginning of his affair with Baladine Klossowska, Rainer Maria Rilke wrote these words to the young poet Franz Xaver Kappus:

There is only one single way. Go into yourself. Search for the reason that bids you write; find out whether it is spreading out its roots in the deepest places of your heart, acknowledge to yourself whether you would have to die if it were denied you to write. This above all—ask yourself in the stillest hour of your night: *must* I write? Delve into yourself for a deep answer. And if this should be affirmative, if you may meet this earnest question with a strong and simple 'I must,' then build your life according to this necessity; your life even into its most indifferent and slightest hour must be a sign of this urge and a testimony to it.[1]

Rilke readily admitted that it is easier to offer advice than to follow it, but in every essential, the life he was to lead until his death in 1926 was an embodiment of the principles he laid out here. Adhering to such principles would entail endless wanderings, sometimes stifling poverty and loneliness, years of poetic inactivity, and a basic lack of fulfillment in love; yet these trials the poet staunchly accepted and endured. Indeed, they came in some way to symbolize for him the outward manifestations of *Verhangnis*—the fated distractions against which he pitted his entire will and being. Very much regarded as a distraction, his love life—for all his protestations to the contrary—was deeply colored and limited by his intense and immutable commitment to his art.

By 1919, this commitment had led Rilke to a very low point in his life. Seven years had passed since his visit to Duino, the castle on the Adriatic belonging to his friend and patron Princess Marie von Thurn und Taxis. It was at Duino, high above the sea on a windswept promontory, that he was inspired to write the first two of what would eventually become ten *Duino Elegies*. As he claimed, the first line—"And if I cried, who'd listen to me in those angelic/orders?"[2]—was literally borne to him as a voice upon the wind. Even as he wrote these first *Elegies*, he had a fully developed conception of the entire cycle, and recognized almost immediately that they were to be his life's work. But the impulse soon faded, and it was in vain that he strove to recapture it. His assertion to Kappus, that "[t]here is here no measuring with time, no year matters, and ten years are nothing" was thus to some extent prophetic, for it would indeed be nearly ten years before the *Elegies* were complete.

From Duino, Rilke resumed his nomadic existence. First to Venice, then to Toledo, seeking as always the elusive *Bereitschaft*—the "readiness" found only in a perfect conjunction of isolation and serenity—necessary for composition. In Ronda he wrote a section of what was to be the sixth Elegy. After a return to Paris, where the distractions of social life brought him to the edge of breakdown, necessitating a trip to Germany for a cure in Rippoldsau, he managed a part of the Third and Tenth Elegies. In 1914 he travelled to Berlin to be with a new love, the pianist Magda von Hattingberg (the "Benvenuta" of his correspondence); when this affair proved, as usual, to be doomed, he journeyed to Leipzig, and it was while he was there that war broke out; he found himself trapped in Germany, a country he had grown to loathe.

The war was disastrous for Rilke, though in fact he wore a uniform for only three weeks in 1916. He did a short stint in the War Archive in Vienna before a petition circulated amongst his influential friends succeeded in winning him an exemption. Nevertheless, the mindlessness of the bloodshed, his own ongoing rootlessness, and another abortive affair helped to quash any hope of serious work, and to deepen the poet's despair over his own lost productivity.

The dissolution of the Austro-Hungarian Empire at the end of the war, and Rilke's subsequent loss of nationality (he was born in Prague and would later become a Czech citizen) seemed to confirm his worst fears of being physically and psychologically homeless. In the aftermath of the unsuccessful communist revolution in Germany, he grasped at a straw proffered by the well-known literary society of Hottingen, near Zurich, which invited him to read. He left Munich, fully expecting a speedy return to Germany.

One of his first visits in Switzerland was to an old acquaintance of pre-war Paris, the artist Elizabeth Dorothee ("Baladine") Klossowska, who, now separated from her husband, art historian Erich Klossowski, was living in Geneva with her two sons, Pierre and Baltusz. The renewed acquaintanceship was enhanced by the bond of shared nostalgia for the good old days. Rilke left shortly thereafter for a triumphant tour of Switzerland, where his poetry was overwhelmingly and universally acclaimed. Travel-weary after the tour, Rilke sought refuge in the mountain village of Soglio, whence he sent the first letter of this collection to Baladine. But Soglio, too, proved unsuited to his purposes, and with the support of his patron Princess Mary Dobržensky he continued to look for a home. The privacy of one that was offered, the house of Schönenberg owned by the Burckhardt family, was inadequate, and he moved on to Venice. When Venice, too, did not seem to offer what he needed, Rilke, sorely pressed as always for funds, resigned himself to a return to Germany. It was on his farewell tour of Switzerland that he paid a last visit to Baladine Klossowska. "As they lingered on her balcony," in the words of Rilke's biographer Donald Prater, something seemed to happen:

though nothing was said, he surprised a tenderness in
her glance that spoke of a stronger bond than friendship,
and in that charged moment there was an awakening of
passion which they would both look back on with emotion.[3]

This is where the story told through the letters in this
collection really begins.

Baladine—or "Merline" as she preferred to be
called—was on her way to visit friends in Beatenberg,
and Rilke to Berne. It was there they met again, and
that, significantly, he adopted for her use his childhood
name of René, with which he was to sign all his correspondence. But their union had in no way altered the
precariousness of his situation in Switzerland; despite
her pleas for him to remain, he had resigned himself to a
return to Germany. At the last moment, however, an
offer came from Richard Ziegler, a friend of Rilke's great
friend and supporter Nanny Wunderly, for the tiny
medieval manor of Berg, a refuge perfectly suited both
to Rilke's tastes and needs. Still he hesitated, consider-
ing instead the offer of an apartment in Geneva, so that
he might stay the winter close to his mistress. While
pondering the decision to be made, he embarked on a
tour of the Valais region with Merline, her husband, and
Klossowski's friends Jean and Frida Strohl; he was particularly struck by the beauty of the region, and would
remember it. Finally though, offered an ultimatum by
the Zieglers, Rilke had no choice but to accept the timely
windfall of Berg. Merline, in turn, aware of his needs,

encouraged this acceptance, "consenting and happy." After a brief but satisfying visit to Paris, Rilke moved into Berg, sustained in all his needs by the generosity of Ziegler, Nanny Wunderly, and others.

At first, the winter in Berg seemed full of promise. As always, in prelude to serious work, Rilke threw himself into an outpouring of correspondence with his friends, patrons and supporters, of which the present collection represents but a tiny fraction. He was not idle creatively, either; he wrote a preface for the published drawings of Baltusz Klossowski (see notes, Letter XI and Letter XXII), and a cycle of ten poems which he entitled *From the Literary Remains of Count C. W.* (in tribute to the ghost that allegedly dictated them to him). Still, these trifles were not the *Elegies*, and the *Elegies* refused to come. What did come was a steady flow of visitors and distractions, not least of which was the news that Merline was suffering in great pain with lumbago. Though in the name of work he resisted the powerful urge to visit her, she eventually spent some time recuperating at Berg. Like Rilke, her finances were in a shambles, and he arranged some help for her and her sons through his patrons. Even so, desperately as she rejected the idea, a return to Germany for her was inevitable, and she finally left for Berlin in April. But the winter had been wasted, his time at Berg had come to end, and Rilke felt that he had betrayed its great promise. For the first time he began to fear that his work would never be completed, and he wrote a "Testament" to that effect, blaming his failure in part on the terrible distractions of love.

He left Berg in May 1921, and stayed in Etoy while he

cast about for a "successor" to Berg. Merline joined him there for the summer, and together they combed the Valais, in southern Switzerland, looking for his new home. They were about to give up when, wandering past a hairdresser's in Sierre, they saw an advertisement of a small manor house for sale or rent. Rilke's instinctive reaction was that this was the place he had been looking for, and with the help of Werner Reinhart, another patron, the Château de Muzot was secured for him. Merline worked tirelessly to make the primitive manor livable, but she knew that she was not to share it if her lover was to achieve his ultimate aim. She hired and trained a new housekeeper, then left for Berlin in November.

Rilke's instincts about Muzot were right—on February 2, 1922, the floodgates were opened. What surged forth, at first, were not the Elegies, but twenty-five sonnets that were to be the first section of the *Sonnets to Orpheus*. These were completed in three days. Immediately thereafter, in an exhausting "hurricane" that was to leave Rilke near collapse, followed four days in which virtually the entire cycle of the *Elegies* was written. Over the next weeks, more sonnets followed, a new Fifth Elegy was written, and Rilke's life's work was accomplished. When he writes "Merline, I am saved!" he is speaking literally, for this few days' work had redeemed all his past failures and vindicated all his many years of tortured self-doubt. It had, in fact, produced one of the masterpieces of 20th century poetry.

Meanwhile, in Berlin, Merline was again ill and in dire financial straits. Her letters to Rilke pleading for help and his presence met with little response. As Prater writes, ''Merline was on her way to become . . . a voice from the past,'' for there was nothing in Rilke's life that had ever been able to compete with his passion for his work. Reinhart's final purchase of Muzot was made on May 12, and Merline joined Rilke there on July 21. Rilke's answer to her announcement of this visit is the final letter in this collection. That summer, she was to quarrel with Frieda, the housekeeper, and attempt in a sense to replace her in her duties and, of course, in her proximity to Rilke. But life with Merline proved enervating and exasperating to the reclusive poet, and he eventually made it possible for her to return to Berlin in November. By that time, early warning signals of the leukemia that was to kill him were already making themselves felt, and Rilke spent the next three years travelling between Muzot, the clinic at Valmont, and various haunts of his old life. He was to see Merline again in the summer of 1924, but by that time they were more old friends than lovers. From Paris, in 1925, they travelled south together to Milan, and it was at the train station in Berne that summer that she saw him last. The next year, dying in Valmont, it was to Merline that Rilke wrote his last letter, on December 23, begging her not to visit him. He died on December 29, and was buried in the hilltop churchyard in Raron. Merline died in Paris in 1969.

As with much of Rilke's verse and prose, these letters are not what they initially appear to be. Whether the reader's interest in Rilke is of a biographical or exegetic

nature (or, of course, both), the important thing to recognize in these letters is that they speak to us not of the
Rilke who had an affair with Baladine Klossowska, but
of the eternal Rilke, the Rilke of the *Elegies,* the Rilke of
whom he himself, in *Self-Portrait 1906,* once had written:

> never in any joy or suffering,
> collected for a firm accomplishment;
> and yet, as though, from far off, with scattered Things,
> a serious, true work were being planned.[4]

—and by extension of all artists who have sacrificed
personal happiness in pursuit of something that would
live beyond their own earthly sufferings.

For a deeper understanding of these letters, one must
accept the fact that Merline was not *the* love of Rilke's
life, nor, despite the coincidence of timing, the inspiration for the *Elegies.* Rather, the love between Rilke and
Merline, and the letters which remain its most concrete
manifestation, represent in every essential the pattern of
Rilke's life, the structure of his thought and instinct, that
enabled him to fulfill what he regarded as his "mission."
And in this capacity, Rilke's letters to Merline are not
only enlightening—they are exemplary.

The only *true* love of Rilke's life—in the sense that it is
the only love which he himself did not thwart, and in
fact went to great lengths to resurrect—was that of Lou
Andreas-Salomé. When they met in Munich in 1897,
Rilke was twenty-one, and Lou, some fifteen years his
senior, was already famous as an author and for her part

in the so-called *ménage à trois* with Paul Rée and Friedrich Nietzsche. As liberated as she was, however, neither Nietzsche, Rée, nor even her husband Friedrich Carl Andreas ever knew her physically. So when she took the young Rilke as her lover, it was a deeply symbolic action, and Rilke recognized it as such. It was the brilliant and enigmatic Lou, more than anyone else in his life, who shaped and ripened his intellect, who taught him application, dedication, observation, and the necessity for sacrifice to creativity. It was she who persuaded him to reject his given name René, and all it represented, for its Germanic version Rainer. And when, her work done, she cast him out into the world, he remained forever devoted and grateful, if somewhat pining.

In essence, Rilke's love life falls into two categories: his love for Lou, and the rest. His first affair, in 1894, was with Valerie von David-Rhonfeld, the "Vally" in his dedication to *Life and Songs*. But already, at nineteen, he was beginning to feel the need for emotional and intellectual independence that was to characterize his approach to his own work, what he would name to Merline as "the awful, inconceivable polarity between life and all-encompassing work." He broke with Vally, herself an artist, in such a way as to emphasize her own (unrecognized) need for a similar independence. Of this affair, Prater writes:

> In its way, the relationship was a prototype of that with all the women in his life: the initial attraction, often to someone older than himself and an artist, the tempta-

tion of a 'normal' life together, the conflict then between the life and his work, with sooner or later—and mostly sooner—the inevitable stern decision that his work must come first, and that he could realize what was in him only in solitude. In an apparently gentle nature, such ruthlessness was surprising.

Surprising though it may have been, this ruthlessness was to be a trademark of all his subsequent involvements, and provides the subtext to all his correspondence with Merline.

Virtually all of his relationships thereafter, including his marriage in 1901 to the sculptress Clara Westhoff, would end in the same way—with Rilke trying, and often succeeding, to convert his mistresses from lovers into devoted friends who would bolster rather than sap his creative energies, who, as he tells Merline, would "become a part and buttress, so to speak, of that tranquility, of that poise which I have so long desired for myself and which (as you know) is the fundamental condition of my life . . ."

The simplistic explanation for such behavior, and one which certainly bears a measure of truth, is that Rilke was exceedingly selfish in his relationships, and cast off his lovers when they had satisfied his needs. But closer to the truth is the fact that none of his lovers ever had, nor probably ever could satisfy his requirements in a partner, which were so lofty, so etherealized, as to reside in a misty, otherworldly plane of intellectual idealism. For his role models, he looked to such historical figures as Sappho, Gaspara Stampa, Bettina von Arnim—the "great lovers," victims of unhappy love affairs who had, in Prater's words, "risen above the need to be loved in return." Indeed, this vision of selfless love comprises a main theme of the First Elegy:

> Shouldn't our ancient suffering be more
> fruitful by now? Isn't it time our loving freed
> us from the one we love and we, trembling, endured . . .

Believing, or at least hoping, with a rather convenient and certainly desperate forgetfulness, that each lover in succession would be the one to fulfill that ideal, or be molded to fit it, he recreated his mistresses in the image of that virtually impossible being. And when they inevitably failed to live up to such standards, when they proved to be normal, sensitive human beings with the basic human needs for requited affection, Rilke was simply confirmed in his abiding conviction that "you could not have both family happiness and art, it must be one or the other—and if art is your choice, then find your happiness there."[5] At that point, he would, as it were, wake up after the shattered dream, and reaffirm his credo, as much to himself as to his understandably bewildered companion:

> Never forget that solitude is my lot, that I must not have
> a need for anyone, that all my strength in fact comes
> from this detachment . . . I *implore* those who love me to
> love my solitude . . .[6]

Plunged again, in the words of Robert Hass, into the "huge raw wound of his longing and the emptiness that fueled it,"[7] Rilke nursed the consolation provided by his altruistic ascetism, his almost messianic sense of self-abnegation for a higher cause. And it was only in this mode—as a sort of secular St. Anthony, retreated into the pure wilderness of his mind and heart where alone he could roam free of temptations—that he was able to hear the voices of inspiration so essential to his creation.

In his relationship with Merline, we find this cycle faithfully regenerated. As with every other woman in his life, his first instinct upon the kindling of passion is that Merline is the one he has been looking for, the perfect "guardian of his solitude." Together, they have entered a "new universe of the soul," it is the "conjunction of two extreme felicities." The story of their love, he tells her,

> is far more beautiful than we can even imagine it; our memory, so swollen by the manifold harvest of this year of blessings, is yet insufficient to hold the entire crop: three quarters of which, you may be sure, remain outside, on the open wind . . .

Or when, in describing the apartment she is shortly to vacate, and in which they spent many a sublime moment together, he waxes Ovidian in ecstatic exaltation of their shared experience:

> I believe that the moment you leave, the gods will transfigure your room amongst the stars, Beloved, and we will occasionally raise our eyes to it . . . It will be a beautiful new star revolving around Venus.

There can be no doubt of his sincerity in these words, or at the very least of his sincere desire to believe them true—though which of these, it is for the reader to decide.

We are given, too, a glimpse of her unrestrained reciprocation, her "happiness all but unknown." In an early taste of her willing subordination to his needs, she tells him: "I am here forever ready, you will find me in every place that you wish me to be with you"—a subordination which, it must be said, Rilke never endeavored to discourage but, on the contrary, manipulated in his efforts to guide the relationship along the desired path. How he does this, and what makes it essentially unnecessary to publish Merline's impassioned responses, is the story told here.

We learn early on that, for all the depth of his love, Rilke has not entirely forgotten his dedication to his mission. "Among the fundamental vows of our love," he reminds her, "was that of never forcing anything, and of bowing to the demands of the moment." To this, as to his other caveats, Merline has consented happily, as she claims, though she had little choice if the relationship was to survive at all. For what Rilke has done— what he had done with Vally, with Clara, with Benvenuta—is to couch his requirements in terms that suggest a mutually beneficial arrangement, one that is as necessary to his partner as to himself. It was clearly a persuasive argument, and one which carried the deepest weight of conviction on his part, for they all seem to have accepted it initially without qualms.

But the (for Merline) artificial structure of the

arrangement soon developed cracks, and its true unilateral nature became readily apparent. She was naturally loathe to be separated from her lover, and at odds to restrain her plaints. "Am I then condemned to make you suffer so much?" Rilke finds himself compelled to ask her. But he is very much prepared, as well, to use the terms of their *mutually* proferred vows in defense of his obstinacy to remain independent. While he admits that he is suffering a "fearful struggle to keep at a distance the most legitimate influences that might sway my clear and firm resolve," he does not hesitate to use guilt to reinforce his position: "What I need now is for you to support me in the decision made: can you do it with an easy heart?" And when she replies, as she must, that she is "consenting and happy" (the reader must assume an emphatically equivocal consent), he is pleased to take this at face value, with no inclination to read between the lines. While she may be sunk in "an abyss of suffering," she is not making a strong enough effort to transcend and thus exalt her suffering, as befits a "great lover." "Having been blessed with such incomparable happiness, should we not then be obliged to aspire to consolations that are no less lofty, no less acute?" Is that too much to ask of her love?

Reading the letters in this way naturally puts their author in a somewhat unflattering, if not to say cruel light. And while of course it is not a critic's place to conceal the truth about his subject, no matter how unpleasant, it must also be said that, apart from the fact that such ruthlessness gave birth to some of the most transcendant poetry of our age, there is ample mitigation to be found within the body of the letters themselves.

We must remember, for instance, that for all his desperate and successful self-protective measures, Rilke did in fact sincerely love Merline, did in fact minister to her physical and financial needs, did in fact compromise to what was for him an unprecedented degree. Furthermore, it is because he took the trouble honestly to document his state of mind for her that we are able to follow the evolution of the *Bereitschaft* that produced the *Elegies*. And there is even evidence to suggest, as Prater does, that "never yet had separation from a mistress caused him such anguish." That such evidence is to be found in abundance in these letters is sufficient in and of itself to place them among the ranks of classic love correspondence.

But what is most integral to the mitigation of Rilke's strange ruthlessness is his steadfast—almost pathological—denial of complicity in it. In his own lights, what made him capable of composing was an obedience to an order higher than himself, an "angel" to which he was enfranchised and beholden for his inspiration. While he never meant this in any literal sense, it does point out the quasi-mystical or prophetic attitude he adopted toward his "mission." Like a visionary or a medium, he struggled endlessly to keep himself pure from disruption and diversion, to descend into the "mine" of distilled experience where no human voice could reach him; in this he had no choice, he "*must* write." It is the attitude that allows him to revere Cézanne for not abandoning his work to attend his own mother's funeral. And it is the attitude that allows him, in all sincerity, to ask Merline: ". . . if our separation were such a great wrong, can you believe that it would have been imposed upon us?" as if he had played no part in its imposition. Again and again throughout the letters, we find this strangely dissociated expression of the relation between his will and his work, one that is based on "devotion and obedience" rather than on the rigorous self-discipline that he himself practiced. It is for him "a greatness of pure destiny, that goes so far beyond us that we are not even allowed to take the blame within it." In its distinction from the personal will, in its insistence on isolation and distance, in its temptation with the fruits of love that can offer the poet no sustenance, it is perhaps more bondage than liberation. Indeed, it might be seen to offer a basis for the interpretation of the chilling portraiture in *The Panther* (1903) that has always been open to ambiguity:

> Only at times, the curtain of the pupils
> lifts, quietly—An image enters in,
> rushes down through the tense, arrested muscles,
> plunges into the heart and is gone.[8]

In such obedience, devotion, and enslavement to a higher decree, one must again make the uneasy comparison between Rilke and an early monastical saint such as Anthony. And while, with or without judgment, one might not expect to find such an outlook amongst one's daily acquaintances, and while it may have run roughshod over lesser personalities, and while it was surely unaware of its own destructive or hurtful capacities, there can be no denying that through its obsessive implementation Rilke was able to create light from the darkness of human pain and suffering. Keeping that in mind while reading these letters, and using it as a constant yardstick by which to measure his capacity both to exalt and manipulate his love for Merline, will help greatly to enhance the reader's appreciation of this remarkable volume, and of its extraordinary author.

Jesse Browner

Notes

1. Rainer Maria Rilke, *Briefe an einen jungen Dichter*. (*Letters to a Young Poet.*) M.D. Herter Norton, trans. New York: W.W. Norton & Co., 1954.

2. Rainer Maria Rilke, *Duineser Elegien*. (*Duino Elegies.*) A. Poulin Jr., trans. Boston: Houghton Mifflin, 1977.

3. Donald Prater, *A Ringing Glass: The Life of Rainer Maria Rilke*. Oxford: Clarendon Press, 1986.

4. Rainer Maria Rilke, "Selbstbildnis aus dem Jahre 1906." ("Self-Portrait, 1906.") From *New Poems,* published in *The Selected Poetry of Rainer Maria Rilke*. Stephen Mitchell, ed. and trans. New York: Vintage Books, 1984.

5. Prater, *A Ringing Glass.*

6. Rainer Maria Rilke, letter to Mimi Romanelli, 1910. Quoted in Prater, *A Ringing Glass.*

7. Robert Hass, "Looking for Rilke." Introduction to Mitchell, ed., *The Selected Poetry of Rainer Maria Rilke.*

8. Rainer Maria Rilke, "Der Panther." ("The Panther.") From Mitchell, ed., *The Selected Poetry of Rainer Maria Rilke.*

Translator's Note

This translation is based on the 1950 edition of *Lettres Françaises à Merline, 1919–1922,* published by the Éditions du Seuil. The forty-two letters of that edition were selected from the complete correspondence, as published later in *Rainer Maria Rilke et Merline: Correspondance* (Zurich: Insel Verlag, 1954). This is the first time that these letters have been translated into English.

Though both Rilke's and Merline's first language was German, they held their correspondence mostly in French, and these letters reflect that preference. About eighty percent of the present text is translated from the French, the rest—generally confined to asides and to concepts that Rilke evidently felt could only be expressed in his native tongue—from the German. The Éditions du Seuil edition renders the original German, and provides footnoted translations; in the interests of clarity and simplicity, the present edition indicates those passages originally in German by placing them in italics.

I would like to express my indebtedness for all bio-graphical material in the introduction and footnotes to Donald Prater's excellent biography, *A Ringing Glass*. I would also like to thank Jacky Marcel Baudot for his invaluable assistance.

J.B.

Letters to Merline
(1919–1922)

Letter I
Soglio (Berghell-Grisons)
August 4, 1919

Dearest *Madame,*

You cannot believe I had forgotten you? Indeed, I am ashamed to be writing you so tardily, but I kept putting off my letter from week to week, waiting for a moment of rest, of truce, so to speak—a moment that is a little beyond the disorder that was essentially master of my days in Switzerland. To be fair, I had some marvelous days in Berne: the historical perseverance of that city was a blessing all the more appreciated in that its civic consciousness, strong and durable evidence of which can still be seen today, presents the most vivid contrast with the middle-class idiocy against which I recently witnessed the struggle of such eager and desperate forces. It is a good thing to remind oneself from time to time that it was this same middle class which, in its youth, erected testimonials of such solemn unity, and was able to express through the medium of an entire city its sober, resolute, and piously definitive character.

Other than these impressions, I was fortunate enough to find some very generous Swiss friends in Berne, which greatly helped my introduction to the true conditions of this difficult country, which you can inhabit for years without knowing any more than its geographical profile and that tiresome, factitious superficiality that is served up in the hostelries. It is true that I almost succumbed to the touristic atmosphere in Zurich, whither I went next with the intention of taking my little cure at the Bircher sanatorium; but my yen for freedom (after five years) was too strong to permit me to submit to such a reclusion. You find me far from there, in Soglio, a little mountain village reached by coach from St. Moritz. A few stone houses, a church at the edge of the precipice, the ancient palace of Salis converted to an inn—that is all of Soglio. Only you must picture it halfway up the mountainside, and provide a panorama of other mountains, snowcapped if you like; but (most importantly) imagine shining above it all a lovely Italian sun (we are barely an hour from the border), and you should know that the slopes are covered with those famous chestnut woods whose spacious and almost sacred beauty may already have been described to you. So much for me. But you, dear lady, where must I envision you? This is not mere phrase-mongering, for I often recall, with an ever-persistent gratitude, those hours that were given me to spend with you; above all, our final evening, as impromptu as it was, has left me with a delicious and enduring memory. The next day, but newly arrived in

Berne, I bought the little book by Louise Labé[1] that I had promised you, and it is only today that I place it in your hands. Understand that I am counting more or less in the increments of eternity, but you will find that some good will come of it. I could not stop myself from buying Masereel's "Book of Hours"[2] that same day; what happiness this rich collection of images has given me! Time and time again I was surprised by its inexhaustible fertility of life and imagination. And it is to you that I owe these treasures.

I trust your charming boys are well?

Write me a few lines, I beg, tell me of your plans and reassure me that I will still find you in Geneva if I arrive later on, after many a peregrination.

Yours in all deference, your

Rilke

1. Louise Labé, c. 1524–1566. French poetess of the Lyons school. Known as "la Belle Cordelière," she was the author of lyrics, elegies, and sonnets, some of which were translated by Rilke. Throughout this edition, translator's notes are numbered, while Rilke's own notes are marked with an asterisk.

2. Frans Masereel, 1889–1972. Belgian artist and illustrator. The book referred to is a "novel in pictures," *Mon livre d'heures* (1919).

Dearest *Madame* and friend,

Two losses I lament, both irreparable: not to have
spent last winter in Geneva—and not to have begged you
on Wednesday: "Stay! Allow one extra day, but one, and
give it entirely to me!" We should have spent it together
from morning to night—it would have left us with a
generous memory. Long as it was, I experienced of our
last evening but the final, ephemeral hours. Anticipation
of our goodbyes was in the air, except during those few
moments we shared leaning upon the balcony—those
were good, extended, and as if above the threat of time.
    You speak true—we do not have enough time to live.
    On Thursday, and the days following, I noticed how
greatly Geneva had changed for me since you left; how
different my days would be if they could end with a visit
to rue X. So, too, has the rue de C.[1] become a rather
nostalgic haunting place for me.

1. The rue de Carouge, where Merline lived.

_____
4

On Friday afternoon, I took myself to Vandoeuvres—but this pilgrimage only served to make me feel your absence all the more.

And we have had rain since yesterday! May your mountain be above these clouds, and equally a little above those others: all the cares that oppress you.

The "port": oh! my dear friend, a certain degree of my apparent tranquility is—alas!—but mere stasis. It is a deceptive port which, lacking communication to the open seas, has become a stagnant pond.

I send up this pilot balloon. You had assured me that a letter simply addressed to B.[2] would reach you; despite my well-justified confidence in the Swiss postal service, I am a little concerned for it: it's only that my Baedecker shows so many hotels in B . . .

—If you should write, don't forget to include an exact address, will you?

May you have pleasant days, and believe, my very dear *Madame,* that I am as you would name me,

> your friend,
> *René*

P.S. I have waited two days to send my missive in the hopes of an exact address. With no news to date, I am sending it anyway on the off-chance.

The weather has improved—but my discomfort persists, and as for everything else, it's the same old thing: I miss you terribly. (Tuesday, August 17.)

2. Beatenberg, near Lake Thun.

Letter III
Bellevue Palace, Berne
Tuesday morning, August 24, 1920

My very dear Friend,

I read and reread your letter so as to be able to grasp that state of mind that no imagination could have foreseen. Darling, your state of heart is infinitely enlarged, and I believe you were not wrong in your initial intention of generously expending it on all those over there who come to you and are deserving of your care. Keep trying—and allow no acoustic, however deceptive, to discourage you—the fact is that we live but an instant (or an eon, who can know?) within a space altogether different from that of actual reality; let me assure you, it is not that your recent words ring false—speak them anyway; but your ear remains tuned to other dimensions.

I know it is difficult, my Friend, to reconcile a "happiness all but unknown" with the current circumstances,

but since in the depths of our being we live on sheer
intensity, how is it that a memory that preserves (so to
speak) the discovery of a new level of intensity of being
should not serve to enrich all your actions and make
them more beneficent than they have ever been before?
Try, try again, have confidence, a rich heart cannot
deceive, do it ingenuously and everyone will be won
over. It seems to me that, with a little shift within yourself, you might exploit your harried strengths to the
attainment of a certain clearsightedness in your current
reflections.

My Friend, I am not sure of finding the right words,
but I feel able nevertheless to bring you some consolation. One must look from the whole to the whole (*vom
Ganzen zum Ganzen*), one must begin at the center, and
since yours, as you told me recently in writing from B.,
has become a tiny sun, you should have little trouble in
turning your face towards it. Reclaim all the serenity
you felt on the Blessed Mountain—or would you have
me worry that we had destroyed that serenity instead of
strengthening it?

As for me, for some time you have made me experience cities, first with you, then without you—an exercise not without its hardships. . . . Listen now:

You must keep me completely up-to-date as to your
plans and itinerary; I may have to remain in Berne a few
extra days, for Mme. de W.[1] has just lost her mother to

---

1. Yvonne de Wattenwyl, a patrician of Berne, Rilke's friend and
sometime benefactor.

an unexpected death, and I believe that in staying here I can be of some comfort, though I barely see her.

If you keep to your intention of returning on the 26th or the 27th (that would be next Friday), I can make arrangements to meet you at the Bellevue instead of risking Zurich and all the obstacles that might eat away at and hinder our time together there. Let me know the moment your plans are settled.

I love your room as if I knew it, and I hope that it will do you some good . . .

And your two hands, I hold them tenderly and I *support* them.

R.

Letter IV
Bellevue Palace, Berne
Monday morning, August 30, 1920

My very dearest Friend,

This morning, I awoke speaking to you (later, you will come to know the words I said to you). I was unable to go on, and I was momentarily overcome.

But how ungrateful it would be to dwell on this; I know, dearest, it is not in sophism that we correct the heart's gravitation, but this gravitation itself has its own laws that we must accept and to which we must submit, in the highest, most sidereal sense.

Having been blessed with such incomparable happiness, should we not then be obliged to aspire to consolations that are no less lofty, no less acute? Let us search for them, dearest, from this moment on let us, in all humility, set out on that good, laborious discovery . . .

For that matter, we began building the foundation of these consolations from our very first evening, and it would be a betrayal of all those paths that brought us together to give in to overwhelming sorrow. Think back, my dearest. Our every conversation was born above adventitious sensations, and it would not be possible that, having enriched ourselves in endless, reciprocal acts of generosity, we should afterwards find ourselves less bold and less wise. One must not become attached to details, even to the dearest of them (that is the way to mutilate the most well-drawn designs of fate). We must refigure the various events of our sensibility within "the whole," for it is only there that they may be judged according to their permanent and definitive worth.

My Friend, think of the diptych of King Andrew that we admired in the museum: even those sad grey stones, even those pearls pierced with golden nails are able to contribute to the general splendor and the exalted harmony of so many beatitudes.

Amongst all the blessings of our "life," there was also that which, side by side with the tender abundance of the moment, provided us with every means to surpass them, not only in the realm of memory, but in the perpetual interpretation of the delights that were granted us.

Dearest, I have just returned from the book store, where I found my pain-ridden book[1] (of prose, begun in Rome, finished around 1910 in my circular room at the Hotel Biron) and the *Sermon on the Love of Magdalena,* an

---

1. *The Notebook of Malte Laurids Brigge* (1910).

---

eighteenth-century work whose author is unknown (attributed by some, rightly or wrongly, to Bossuet). As to the other old book, the *Malte*, I have often had to take it away from young people, forbidding them to read it. For this book, which seems pretty near to demonstrating the conclusion that life is impossible, must be read *against the grain*, as it were. If it contains bitter reproaches, it is not against life that they are aimed; on the contrary, it represents the continual recognition that it is through lack of strength, through distraction and inherited mistakes that we lose almost entirely the countless riches of the present that were our birthright.

My dearest, try to overlook the effusiveness of these pages in that understanding—it will not spare you weeping, but it will help to give your tears a clearer and, so to speak, more transparent meaning.

Your friend,
René

P.S. Overleaf you will find the verses which I composed for you on Saturday while strolling through the wonderful avenue of Hollingen castle.

Letter V

Bellevue Palace, Berne
Tuesday morning, August 31, 1920

Dearest, Dearest,

How many times must I write "Dearest" so as nearly to fill the measure of this great, swollen heart you left me?

Dearest, I grew a little anguished last night as I waited for your telegram—but in the end your kind letter, which was brought to me around half-past nine, was ample reward. I read it and reread it right up until I fell asleep . . .

I too spend moments behind my hands, so as to feel nothing but the contents of my heart, enlarged, magnified, infinitely multiplied.

I have just sent you a telegram to inform you that I am extending by one day my stay at the Bellevue. I am reluctant to be away from you even a few hours more. And yet I am joyously moved by the idea that in Zurich I will meet with those who love you . . .

The spray of your gladioli is opening ever more magnificently: of its eleven flowers, seven have bloomed as if out of pride, and within their chalices glows a fiery interior, an imaginary red space that passionately, almost tragically deepens the room.

This morning, I bought for the writing desk a few more roses, young, bright, matinal, as matinal as the gladioli are nocturnal, volcanic and flaming.

Dearest, goodbye. I kiss your letter at length, religiously; it too will be kept in its entirety in that happy treasury I keep behind my closed eyes. And I will copy out the passage that holds your great, your generous promise: "I am here forever ready, you will find me in every place that you wish me to be with you." I will recopy it to keep in my wallet as a talisman.*

From now on, you'll have brief news, keeping you always up-to-date on where I can be found; I hope to be able to apply some energy to the pursuit of the path I have laid out for myself, arduous as it is. And I wish myself in the hands of God as you have placed me in his care.

your friend,
René

* No, copy it for me, in your hand, it will be all the stronger; I could tear it from your letter but it would pain me to destroy it.

13

Letter VI
Baur au Lac, Zurich
Friday, September 17, 1920

Friend, oh my Friend,

Am I then condemned to make you suffer so much? I beg of you, call a short truce with your pain, and look: this is still life, the very same that carried us to the peaks of our hearts. You cannot accuse it of cruelty without at the same time charging it with having been so generous.

Fortunately, the double letter I sent you Wednesday will have reached you yesterday; has it lightened your ordeal a little? Oh, if only, by caressing the paper between my hands, I were able to transmit some of that infinite tenderness of which I have never been able to give you enough; I even wonder whether in fact you have had any, my hands having remained, Dearest, so inexhaustibly brimming with it. In keeping silent I had hoped that, all unprompted, you would take up our accumulated wealth and put it to the greatest variety of

14

uses. That is what you must try to do; it is what I compel myself to do, as best I can; we receive such blessings only at the price of a firmer commitment to life, and we must glorify it, even through our tears. Try, my Friend, act upon what you have become, summon up the curiosity to know and to use your new heart straight from the crucible of metamorphosis innumerable! You will gradually gain strength as you summon it. Soon there will be a lull, and even a sense of well-being.

Sweet Friend, I leave for R.[1] in two hours, I think I may stay until Monday—I will keep you informed of all my movements . . .

I carry with me still the little handkerchief steeped in your tears; I carry it as a symbol that all of your tears, Friend, all of your tears will forever dry on my heart . . .

And allow me to believe, my Love, that I sustain you day and night, and that you never feel for one moment that I have abandoned you,

René

1. Possibly Ragaz, one stop on Rilke's tour of Switzerland.

Letter VII
Baur au Lac, Sunday
Zurich, September 26, 1920

Dearest, oh Dearest,

I have dismantled an entire rose with which to furnish for you this little book of Bettina's,[1] which I was only able to find (in the fourth bookstore) in this mediocre edition (this book, which is capable of doing so much good, is not amongst those one tears from oneself). Moreover, it is the same edition in which I have always read it, how many times! As for *Malte*, I had managed with great difficulty to buy a lovely original (now rare) which has since been lost along with all the books from the rue Campagne-Première which, in part, was the library of *Malte* . . .[2]

1. The *Correspondence* (*Briefwechsel mit Einem Kinde*, 1835) between Bettina von Arnim (1785–1859) and Johann Wolfgang von Goethe.

2. The entire contents of Rilke's Paris apartment was auctioned off by the French authorities in April 1915.

This Sunday morning, while all the bells in the two "Münster" spread a sort of rich aerial brocade over Zurich, I allowed myself to share a little in the life of the "Briefwechsel"; how many sublime passages I should have liked to mark for you—but you will discover them, beloved, by the very instinct of love—and you'll find that it was not at random that I inserted and distributed these delightful petals. On the page where Günderode shows her troubled friend the spot beneath the heart where one can kill oneself, I have placed a rose-petal sorrowfully stained. What a lover was that Bettina: never was a bold heart so near to a heroic spirit, and yet neither suppressed nor modified its inexpressible fervor in turn, but rather, *returned it*!

I have just passed beneath the ancient covered bridge that leads toward the station. I went there purposely, Beloved, to be sure of walking where once your feet alit with pleasure and gentle curiosity. Oh, to think they came my way!

René

Letter VIII
Tuesday, September 28, 1920

My very dearest,

Tell me, have I been such a poor support to you that, despite all my loving assistance, you should have allowed yourself to sink to such an awful distrust of life? I am not reproaching you with it, I merely suffer with you, and not wishing to make the useless effort of deceptive consolation, I tell you that I understand.

No one could understand as I do your sense of oppression, your anguish, and how at times you have felt yourself abandoned by those powers which yet have been multiplied by the joining of our blazing lives. My Friend, if our separation were such a great wrong, can you believe it would have been imposed upon us? What confounds it is that we both find ourselves incapable of enriching it with the very real consequences of our prodigious happiness. If you were alone at present (as you yourself wrote the other day), you might have evolved a wholly different consciousness, courageous and willing. I too, through lack of solitude and concentration, am in a muddle; I need to see people and to talk throughout the day; at twilight I take refuge in the hotel garden, I stay there for hours and at times I fly towards you with such boldness of heart that I can no longer tell whether I am doing you good or evil with my relentless approach. When, my Friend, will we be able to master the violence of these irresistible urges? Let us mutually implore one another to offer, with our sometimes too outstretched hands, a little sweet respite.

You ask me again about my lengthy stay here: it is entirely taken up with my preparation of means to remain in Switzerland, if only for a few more weeks. Some friends are quite disposed to setting me up, by myself, in an ancient little castle a few hours from Z., which would be relatively comfortable even in winter; but being able to secure funds neither from Austria nor from Germany, I see no way to provide for the necessities of my existence there.[1] We are still negotiating certain arrangements toward that—and I feel rather torn asunder by it all. My responsibility to my life, disrupted and disfigured by these past years—to my work, which, for want of continuity and stability no longer belongs to me, has become so burdensome, that I know that I must not be dismayed by even the hardest decisions. I should

---

1. The German mark was in its postwar decline. Though Rilke had an ample account with his publisher in Munich, the money sent to him, when converted to Swiss francs, had little value.

choose my spot according to its promise for my work, so long neglected—and it is a fearful struggle to keep at a distance the most legitimate influences that might sway my clear and firm resolve. I sometimes come away from it ripped to shreds, but I keep telling myself that among the fundamental vows of our love was that of never forcing anything, and of bowing to the demands of the moment. In effect, by taking this nascent happiness into our own hands, so to speak, we might well be the first to destroy it; it must remain on the anvil of its Creator, beneath His painstaking hammer blows. Let us place our poor trust in that admirable Artisan. It is true, we will forever feel the shocks of His tool pitilessly wielded according to the rules of a perfected art; but in return we will also be called upon from time to time to admire His favorite work wrought to ultimate perfection: how we admired it once before, that first time! We are but barely participants in our own love; and it is in that very thing that it will remain above commonplace dangers. Let us try to learn its laws, its seasons, its rhythms, and the progress of constellations across its vast, starlit sky. Let us stay, my Friend, stay and admire!

I am well aware that in speaking to you in this manner, we have altogether unequal tasks thrust upon us: you are too much of a woman not to suffer endlessly from the suspension of love which seems to lie in this task. And I, in closing myself in upon my work, am assuring the means of my most definitive well-being; whereas you, at least for the moment, in turning to your life, find it burdened with duties halfway paralyzed. Do not let it discourage you, my very dearest one; it will all change, you see. The transfiguration of your own heart will gradually come to bear upon the unyielding givens of reality; all of that which seems to you opaque, you will make transparent with your blazing heart. . . . For the time being, think not much upon it, and forbid yourself to judge life during these fog-bound times that allow you no sight of its sweeping panorama.

Tell me anyway of your plans, my darling—God knows whether they are as infeasible as you believe. Tell me all the more as, with my own, I find myself in a bleak, blind alley which I would not care to leave without having at least stirred up a few new ideas, even imaginary ones.

"The little bunch of roses" arrived only yesterday, Monday morning. It belonged to me in its every significance . . .

René

Letter IX
Bellevue Palace, Berne
Sunday, October 17, 1920

Most dear Friend,

Am I going to cause you pain? I have first caused
some for myself; an hour ago, I wrote to S.,[1] to break
our appointed meeting on rue X.

But newly arrived in Berne, I was forced to review my
winter plans, for I found here some photos and detailed
information about B. castle; the owner will shortly be
leaving and I was asked to make a definite, final decision. I gave it some thought: its advantages are such
and, in giving them a second consideration, I have been
unable to banish the conviction that it is surely the

---

1. The architect Guido von Salis, a recently made friend. Salis had
arranged Rilke's tenancy, to begin November 1, in a small apartment
in Geneva.

retreat I have sought for so long. It is a fortuitous gift; I must accept it.

I foresee that my stay in Paris will further increase my longing for a complete and extended solitude, for in coming again upon my former life so cruelly disrupted, I shall find myself committed to undertaking great efforts toward continuity. I believe I shall be able to pursue them under the reclusive conditions afforded better by this ancient abode than elsewhere . . .

I know I would offend you, Beloved, if I made as if to justify myself in your eyes. If I repeat the reasons for my reversal, it is certainly not so as to force them upon you; it is to bolster and convince myself.

Furthermore, please do not start believing that my earlier decision to settle in Geneva was taken by order of your influence; my freedom in revoking it should prove to you that I was just as free in my commitment to it. For that matter, you were a witness to my doubts, and you may have felt that, beneath the surface, they continued to trouble me . . .

What I need now is for you to support me in the decision made: can you do it with an easy heart? I am counting on you terribly, my wonderful Friend: send an "express" message to me at B. I will be arriving there tonight. I will send you pictures of Berg Castle and we shall have time to discuss all this, for from Paris I will be returning to Geneva, and will stay there until everything is ready for my move to Berg's serene refuge.

I am concerned that I may have left S. in an unpleasant situation. Will he begrudge me? My very dearest, I

23

am sending you this news in all haste—may you not find it too awful. I am so anxious to speak with you, to hear you, to feel you, and what saddens me so much at this moment is being unable to put across on paper all the transports of confidence that carry me toward you, my infinite heart.

René

Letter X
October 19, 1920
Tuesday, two o'clock

Yesterday, at this very hour, you were writing that dear, dear letter, my wonderful Friend, consenting and happy: for that you must be, since you were able to write as you have. Oh, how good it is, Dearest, what you tell me, those comforting words of love, for it seems to me that in this alone we surpass anything that this winter in Geneva might have given us; we lose nothing, we persist in the unity we would have reached by living in the same city through those arduous months. It is like a shortcut to life—Dearest; we will never lose anything, for all our sacrifices will be accepted by that same God who protects us, and it is up to us to enrich it every now and then with our wise privations.

My very Dearest, this morning I received my visa to Paris from the French consulate; thanks to the recommendations with which I armed myself, I was treated there with every possible respect.

Imagine that amongst all the many letters and parcels that have not been forwarded, I have found André Gide's *Symphonie Pastorale*, which he sent along with a kind and sincere dedication. So he is the first to give me my little auspicious omen, and I shall not waste any time in approaching him with open heart. Still, if only it had arrived earlier!

If all goes well, I shall leave Wednesday or Thursday evening.

Goodbye, my very Dearest—how sweet it is for me to go to France and to love Paris this time with all my infinite feeling, and with yours that I take with me.

René

Letter XI
Schloss Berg am Irchel
November 18, 1920, Thursday

No, I am not at all surprised to find you so strong;
what is now giving you courage is that very same freedom that allowed you to enter the sanctuary of our love
and to kneel, not as a mere worshipper but as high
priestess who, in her deliciously experienced arms,
raises to God the ultimate offering. So too would you be
wrong, Beloved, not to offer your whole heart for my
adoration; alone with it, you shall uncover talents in it
that were hitherto unknown—it is only now that you
can take possession of it, simultaneously new and more
familiar, no longer a waxing heart, it will be completely
full, round, the planet—which will bathe you in the rays
of your childhood and the first bloom of youth.

Harvest love's first harvest, work to fill the soul's
granary with the brimming crop we brought to season

with our tireless warmth. I, the "image hunter," go up into my mountains, wild, taciturn, losing myself. But you, my delicious valley, you, my heart's flute, you, earthenware vase on whom I, love's humble artisan, bestowed the inspired curve that consecrated you forever to divine usage—you, who have the innate, imperturbable patience of the landscape and the flute and the holy chalice! May you succeed, my love, in abandoning yourself to the rhythms of the seasons and of the mouth and of the hand. Let us not be satisfied with recounting a fable of the heart; let us create its myth. Is not love, with art, our only license to overreach the human condition, to be greater, more generous, more sorrowful if need be, than is the common lot? Let us be so heroically, my sweet friend—let us give up not one advantage afforded by our spirited state of being.

Since this solitude closed in around me (and it was absolute from the very first day), I am experiencing yet again the awful, inconceivable polarity between life and all-encompassing work. How far from me is the work, how far the angels!

I will shuffle slowly ahead, each day moving forward but a half-step, and often losing ground. And with each step will I seem to leave you farther behind, for where I am going no name has any value, no memory can remain; one must reach it as one reaches the dead, in consigning all one's forces to the hands of the Angel who leads you. I am leaving you behind—but as I will be making full circle, I will again draw nearer with each step. The bow is strung to let the arrow fly at the heavenly bird; but if it falls to earth, it will have passed harmlessly through the bird, and it will fall from on high into your heart.

Please do not expect me to speak to you of my inner labor—I must keep it silent; it would be tiresome to keep track, even for myself, of all the reversals of fortune I will have to undergo in my struggle for concentration. This sudden shifting of all one's forces, these about-faces of the soul, never occur without many a crisis; the majority of artists avoid them by means of distraction, but that is why they never manage to return to the center of their productivity, whence they started out at the moment of their purest impulse. At the onset of every work, you must recreate that primal innocence, you must return to that ingenuous place where the Angel found you, when he brought you that first message of commitment; you must seek through the brambles for the bed in which you then slept; this time you won't sleep: you will pray, wail—anything; if the Angel condescends to come, it will be because you have persuaded him, not with your tears, but by your humble decision always to start afresh: *ein Anfanger zu sein!*[1]

Oh my Dearest, how many times in my life—and never more than now—have I told myself that Art, as I perceive it, is a movement against nature. God probably never foresaw that any of us would take this awful plunge into himself, which would have been permitted only to the Saint, since he aspires to lay siege to his God by attacking Him from that unexpected and poorly defended flank. But we, on whom then are we advanc-

1. "To be a beginner!"

ing when we turn our backs on events, on our own
future, so as to hurl ourselves into this abyss of our being
that would swallow us whole? Did we not bring to it
that strange faith which seems stronger than the urgings
of our own nature? If the notion of sacrifice is that the
instant of greatest danger coincides with that of redemp-
tion, there is certainly nothing more closely resembling
sacrifice than the terrible will of Art. How headstrong it
is, how senseless! All that others forget so as to make life
bearable, we forever go and seek out, magnify even; we
are the true awakeners of our monsters, whom we do
not sufficiently oppose to vanquish, for, in a certain
sense, we agree with them; it is they, these monsters,
who hold the excess of strength vital to those who must
overreach themselves. Unless we attribute a mysterious
and far deeper meaning to the act of victory, it is not for
us to claim ourselves walking side by side with them, as
in a triumphal procession, without being able to recall
the precise moment when this inconceivable reconcilia-
tion took place (a barely arching bridge that connects
the terrible to the tender . . .)

Dearest, I will speak no more to you about all this. . . .
I am taking a vow of silence, and if, occasionally, rarely,
I send you a little sign of life, I will speak rather of my
surroundings, of the visible, of the "framework" of my
current life. As to this, it is perfect, it lacks nothing either
in my comfort or in the silence of this solitary retreat.
The simple, serene castle, full of that assurance given by
ancient abodes that have had the time to develop the
consciousness of a home. The rooms required very little

rearranging. An enormous writing table has taken the place of the little bench that stood by the windows. The dining table is in the middle of the room by the great leather sofa that faces the fireplace, where I sit to read. Everything is simpler than the maps seem to indicate, more solemn and more evocative. The park itself, as it appears from the window, has a more rustic feeling to it, all the more so as it opens out completely at one end and as, beyond the last avenue, it gives way to the meadows that rise in gentle slopes to the "Irchel": this modest wooded hill softly defines the horizon without cluttering it too much. The principal role falls to the fountain which, with an almost statuary flourish, rises in the middle of her rimless pond. It is she who chats with me day and night; even through the closed windows comes the hint of her vital song limiting the silence! At night, from my bed, I am even able to distinguish through the open window every nuance of her tumbling waters, modulated by their least change in cadence. And imagine this: this faithful fountain, which seems placed not within an enclosed park but in the very bosom of nature, thrusts herself upon me like a vision from the *Metamorphoses*. Could it be your heart that endlessly rises and falls before me in its secure happiness? . . . The moment this idea came to me, I asked if the water were switched off in the winter. No, the fountain will always run: always it will support the vault of my gaze with its lively double pillar, and always will its whisper enter my ear to form the constant weft to the fabric of my dreams.

But before closing I have a few other details I would like to take up. The little basket I had sent to you will have revealed that I found one myself for your lovely embroidery. Yours was greatly fussed over by the vendor, who took it back a number of times to look more closely at it, expressing the pleasure she felt over this gentle piece of work. The basket I bought is quite simple, your little work just about covers the bottom: it is still on my table, filled with *zwieback*;[2] bread would be too heavy for your leaves and your flowering little name.

Beloved: without telling him, embrace B.[3] for me. I am sorry not to have done it myself; it's one of those silly discretions one scolds oneself for afterwards. When I return, I will do it, with all the tenderness I feel for him. I spoke with his publisher by telephone; we're going to draft the contract sometime soon, only I alone will append my signature, because B., being a minor, cannot enter into any contract.

How you showed me Geneva beneath that clement and still generous sky! Here, too, an indescribable gentleness that seems at times more like a moment of spring than the thoughtful meditation of autumn. The russet tones of hedgerows dominate the countryside and the very air, which here tends more to gold than to that silvery clearness we so love. I rarely go out, for fear of upsetting my efforts of concentration that are better

---

2. Rusks.

3. Merline's son, Arsène Davitcho Klossowski, called "Baltusz." Rilke would soon write the preface to accompany a series of forty drawings by the eleven-year-old boy, and the collaboration, entitled *Mitsou*, was to be published in Zurich with Rilke's help. Baltusz was later to achieve world fame as an artist, signing his work "Balthus."

served in the house than in any other surrounding. In any case, most of the roads are closed because of foot-and-mouth disease, such that I am a prisoner of the park and of my own castle.

Dearest, I am slow—I have been writing you since this morning and my clock has just chimed four o'clock. I am thinking of you, my very Dearest—you have closed behind you that door at which I waited and skulked for someone I was expecting. It was this anxiety that kept disturbing me. I no longer feel it. I sense your arrival, and it has made my heart overflow.

René

Letter XII

Schloss Berg am Irchel
Canton of Zurich
November 22, 1920, Monday, five o'clock

Merline,

I have just come in from the park, green, brown, all warm under a barely perceptible rain whose dry little noise I heard on my stroll as it fell upon the desiccated leaves strewn over the path, upon the boxwood borders, and the pale-green cabbages in the kitchen garden—I come in, light my lamp (it has been a day for letters which, in their great numbers, have somewhat distracted me from my thoughts of work). But before I have time to reflect on what remains to be written this evening, my heart drags me towards you with such a powerful undertow that I give myself over to it unresisting—forever. This heart, my Friend, has stayed awake these past nights while I slept, continuously filling me with tenderness such that I held my arms against my chest as if to provide some resistance to this overflowing and almost annihilating feeling of gentleness. It is in that position that I awake in the morning.

How pleased I am for that great soulful emotion that you brought away from *Hamlet*! You know how unrestrained are my expectations of Pitoëff[1] whenever he is able to draw on his instinct for Art and that admirable vision, both extremely intense and strong, which allow him to appropriate works within the scope of his imagination. I have just sent him a short congratulatory message, for the resonance I felt in your voice has forever glorified his wonderful triumph for me.

Yesterday I was leafing through those little notebooks that contain my diary entries since I arrived in Switzerland; I opened the very first, and found your name on the fifth page. There I make note of my arrival in Geneva, I mention the circular bench behind the cathedral where I had lunch and—you! Think, these were my first moments in Switzerland. Doesn't it seem as if I knew my heart's goal? And yet, no, I was not aware that I had arrived so propitiously.

René

---

1. Georges Pitoëff. Russian emigré, actor, founder of an international theater in Geneva, and a close friend of Rilke.

Letter XIII
Saturday night

I have just come from the park.

Strolling up and down the hornbeam avenues, I summoned you, Merline, I was almost able to *see you*! Hot tears, such as I have never known before, came to my eyes, and I was as if dazzled by the feeling that unites us, Merline, by the trust, by the abiding friendship that underlies a profound love. That such a thing could exist, and that it was given us to experience it—*to us*, Merline, to us, to Merline and to

René

P.S. And now, when outdoors, I always wear the gloves that you washed for me, and when I take them off, my hands smell of your hands, your soap, your little washbasin, and the air on your balcony!

Saturday night (a little later)

After the evening post: your letter of yesterday, dated "Friday afternoon," the second I have received today, and this one altogether *you,* serene, loving, tender and intimate. Oh, Merline, I am ashamed; how I chastise myself for my irritability, my weakness, and also for all those letters written yesterday and this morning that are travelling your way! You will be appalled by me when you receive them; one more—my Friend, I have suffered, but I recover as quickly as you, I have kindled a marvelous fire in my fireplace, the first in eight days, and in the flickering of the passionately burning logs, I am looking at *your pastels in love with everything* that I have just unpacked; it is a light that makes them almost too bewitching—one is lost in them, it's magical, there can be no resistance. The golden hair of the young girl at the balcony in springtime takes on a sensual vibrancy, really an entire pubescent season that exploits it to seduce. And the girl, thinking that it's only she—*everything crackles in these pastels like the flames in the fireplace, the darknesses are aglow and the luminosities darken as on a northern summer's eve. And all that is contained on a page is somehow inexpressibly felt as simultaneous, not one after the other, you understand; that is what gives these drawings their quality as ''images.'' Like a breeze passing over a bed of coals,* a unique breath *has passed over each of these relationships, kindling some, stifling others, and that is precisely what constitutes the secret event that connects them.* I could write you pages and pages on the ballgame, a marvelous correspondence between the two gestures, of the boy in the background and the little girl, and between these two expressive states, the lovely red ball, instinctively *there* where it is flying, moving, rejoicing in its independence. The *Woman at Her Mirror*, very rich, very dreamlike; and how her arm, handing the flowers to the one arranging them on her motionless head, perpetuates itself in the other arms whose slow, hesitant task we "know," where randomness mingles with dream, and the concentration of arrangement with a wholly feminine abstraction. And the sumptuous music of the lines enveloping this silence, primping and preparing!

The *Girl at the Window* (if only I could believe it mine!), one of those windows we talked about in Fribourg, no, a hundred, a thousand windows in one—a tragic frame to this gesture which, in raising up her hair, seems to form the image of a cry. Arm, oh arm! . . . A body modeled as if from afar. And in such a perfect "knowledge," *voluptuously known,* that hastily sketched line that traces the contours of her blouse, a line that grows hot and rises, all flustered, to the arm!

And the sleeping woman! *The pretty woman asleep,* yes, as a woman she is pretty, as a little work of art she is sublime! My God, how she sleeps, it's a translation of all her lineaments "in sleep," how she droops, and yet, at the last minute, the two hands she has placed beneath her lovely, dozing, silken head, receive and support all her weight transfigured as unconscious sleeper. It is a magic spell, Merline, and in this: the delicious presence of all those lines, indispensable accessories not provided to fill up space, but to complement, to collaborate, to clown a little while sleeping in the empty air that surrounds sleeping people. You are led everywhere by an infallible instinct; I marvel at those few stains of color with which you hinted at the bed; and that scarlet by her head which renders her even more "unconscious!"

(Saturday at 9:30)

(Sunday night)

All those little pages, Beloved, I wrote you yesterday in a state of exhaustion, but also of relief, which almost made me dizzy, and today I have designated as a day of rest, without, however, allowing myself any great freedom. I wrote five or six letters that were weighing on me; there's no end to it, for I have been sorely delinquent on all counts. Little by little I return to the level of the current, but all this tiring forced labor is what continually restrains me at the very threshold of real work.

—In Friday's letter, my Friend, you express a sweet and tender curiosity to know how *I* am faring. I am well. I am, it is true, extremely tired, to the point where I sometimes don't rise until 9:30 in the morning, so tardy an hour that I am ashamed to confess it. As far as I can remember, I have never given myself to such laziness; I have always needed a lot of sleep, especially during the days focused inward, but then my habit of going to sleep about the same time as the chickens allowed me to begin my day, if not with them, at least with the domestic chores that also have their appointed rising hour. Now, the chairs and cupboards and tables have been waiting for me for quite a while, and scold me when I rise. I must nevertheless take the blame. For at times my room, my large workroom, is so kind to me at night, so enwrapping, that I can't bring myself to leave it; I light the fire, I sit with my book, I contemplate, I delay endlessly while drinking with all my senses that indescribable silence that scared me as a child but which loves me now, and more, is preparing me for I know not what, but I might guess, for my purest labor.

As to work—I am drawing nearer, but slowly. And it is my own temperament that is slowing me down, stopping me. It has been so long since I have lived on the hearth of my work that I find it quite cold and, in order to rekindle it, I require a heat so intense and spontaneous that to produce it I withdraw my blood from all my organs to deploy it in my heart and in my head, and then the poor stomach starts to complain, bereft as it is of all interest—the mealtime hours bother me, seem like an annoying interruption, and naturally my discomforts make themselves felt and, in the end, are much more troublesome than the shifting of attention one has to make in sitting down to table. I am aware of all this and do not rest for sincerely berating myself—and without any perceptible result. This approach to work disturbs my temperament with an almost elemental violence, and it is practically beyond the power of my will to soothe nerves jolted by the electrical charges of imagination and inner voices.

To all these extraordinary circumstances L.[1] has adapted marvelously. She is hardly ever there, she never asks any questions and seems to be shocked by nothing. With all that she takes perfect care of me, I barely need to see her in person, she has, somehow, an atmospheric presence, and I'm not certain that I shouldn't keep her with me for a long time to come. Imagine, it has been like this since the first day.

Henceforth, I would like to live forever outside of chance. This pure solitude! No one watching you, aware of what is going on within you and, in that alone, already imposing themselves and meddling in your purposes. Chance: I mean all those futile encounters, all that awkward chitchat, all that throws itself upon you in idleness, in fortuity even, crude chance, in a word, that we know so well and that sometimes disposes of us for hours, indeed, for an entire day. I want no more of such chance. It is only appropriate in Paris, since there, where one's options are limitless, it becomes prodigal and even inspired, and since in a completed world it becomes elemental—no longer producing incidents—it creates constellations!

My Very Dearest, what more did I have to tell you? Everything. Nothing has yet been told you, everything is still to tell and, after everything, everything will still remain, for we are not concerned with what is accountable between us, but what is inexpressible and infinite, which will never begin. We show it to each other—look!

1. Rilke's housekeeper, Leni Gisler.

My Friend, goodnight. You are doing better, almost well, for certain?

My next parcel to be sent after this one will be registered, because of the notebook containing the recopied letters, and the photos from the Valais.

Your pastels enchant me, Beloved! It hurts me to abandon them to the threat of being sold. My God, who will love them?

René

Letter XIV
Schloss Berg am Irchel
Canton of Zurich
December 16, 1920, Thursday

Oh my Friend,

I, too, in reading, rereading and reading again your long and tender letter last night in the corner of my hearth (I knew that all these preparations for "the climb" would be too uprooting for you, and now you are going to work at Christmas), Beloved, *I beg of you* (still to the same tune), arrange yourself a little rest beforehand, a *ceasefire,* I solemnly beg you, prolong by a few days this most peaceful of Sundays, do so, my Friend—*it is of the greatest importance that you be well for Christmas.*

As for me, I promise to behave myself and to pay a little more attention to the dishes my taciturn country-woman sets before me; you know I am not amongst those who neglect the body so as to make it an offering to the soul—mine should not appreciate being treated in that way. Moreover, all my spiritual impulse springs from my blood; that is why a simple, wholesome life, free from excitants and stimulants, must be prelude to my work, so that I cannot mistake the true spiritual joy that consists of a joyous and somehow glorious harmony with all of nature. Only, I find myself in such an unusual situation inwardly because of that lengthy, forced hiatus and because I must return to those emotions which, while very worthy, nevertheless bear the date of 1912. A little longer and I may lose all understanding of the conditions under which these songs, begun so long ago, arose. If one day you come to know these works, you may understand me better; it is so difficult to explain.

When I scrutinize my conscience I see but one law, and that pitilessly categorical: to shut myself away within myself, and in one blow to finish the task that was dictated to me in my heart's core. I obey, for you know well that in coming here that is all I wanted, and I have no right to change the direction of my will before having completed my act of devotion and obedience!

Oh no, it was not as you said, as you called me in your earlier letter, "too selfish"—I assure you, it was also and to the highest degree "selfless." If I imagine going to Geneva for no other reason (without even venturing onto rue P.J.[1]) than to accompany you to your grocer's on rue de Carouge . . . and if, after having greeted every-

1. The rue du Pré-Jerome, around the corner from Merline's apartment on rue de Carouge.

one there, I were to return to the station and come back here . . . if I imagine only that, *that alone seems to me such happiness, such bliss,* even were we not to talk, even were you to scold me for some reason or another . . . Beloved: use this sentiment as your yardstick, and know, measure by it how "selfless" it would be to ask me to return . . .

But, oh Dearest! How agreeable I know you to be, that in yesterday's letter you encouraged me, bravely and boldly, *to stay!* With those few words, which did not seem too disheartened, you lifted my heart and lowered it again where it lay once more, on the altar where it must burn for a few months longer. Oh, if it were possible for my feeling for you to grow any larger, at that instant I felt in it a fullness such that I had to close my eyes and wrap myself in my own arms (as during that night of which I told you) to contain it. Yes, beloved, help me in this heroic way, mold yourself to this serene landscape, these quiet walls that protect me, protect me with them—be, oh be that fountain which all this time has been insisting: "stay, stay . . ." I am here, I set the example of that shift you must make within yourself . . . And if, in descending into the depths of my work, a dark miner lost to the light, I send you but rare, laconic messages, little signs from a hunter who must keep silent in his blind so as not to frighten the precious game that approaches . . . do not be saddened, my sweet darling, do not feel yourself abandoned, forsaken, forgotten. Think that there where I shall be buried, I will be approaching your heart from the opposite direction, as it were, silently—for how close were our heights to that sublime axis where my toiling fervor burns!

My very dearest, I long so much to enfold you in my arms, they open at all moments, without my realizing it, and if your tenderness has been embodied beside you (oh, I have seen it, seen it), I swear to you that mine fills all the space between us, and all that surrounds you to the very limits of your vision, all that you breathe, *is my tenderness for you,* you may be certain of it.

I have just about finished all the *Vorarbeiten,* that is to say the awful backlog of my correspondence—imagine (I have just counted them this morning), I have written 115 letters, not all of the length of that to General S.,[2] but not one of less than four pages and many of eight or even twelve, in a rather cramped hand. (Of course, I am not counting all those I sent to you. That is not writing; it is breathing through the pen.) So many letters! Oh, Beloved, there are so many people who expect I know not what from me—help, advice (from me, who am so terribly *rathlos*[3] before the most urgent necessities of life!), and though I know that they are wrong, that they deceive themselves—I am nevertheless tempted (and I don't think by vanity!) to pass on to them some of my experiences—some fruits of my extended solitude . . . in the same sense in which I did so for that blind man. I see

---

2. Major-General Cäsar von Sedlakowitz, Ret. As a First Lieutenant, Sedlakowitz had been Rilke's German teacher at the St. Pölten Junior Military Academy. He had recently written to Rilke, congratulating him on his success and recalling younger days. In October 1920, Rilke had replied with a long letter describing his deep misery during his time at the Academy.

3. Helpless.

that you were moved by that letter; I was not wrong, then, to write it . . . And women and young girls horribly alone even in the bosom of their families—and young brides frightened by what has befallen them . . . and then all those young people, workers, mostly revolutionaries, who come disoriented out of the state prisons and stumble through "literature" while writing the poetry of nasty drunks . . . What to tell them? How to raise up their despairing hearts, how to mold their twisted wills that, by force of events, have taken on a borrowed and wholly temporary personality, and which they now carry about them like alien powers that they scarcely know how to use!

My experiences with *Malte* sometimes compel me to answer these strangers' cries; he himself would have done it, if ever such a voice had reached him—and he has left me a sort of inheritance of action that I am unable to divert from its charitable destination. Moreover, he is the one who compels me to persist in this boundless devotion, who makes me love all the things I wish to create with all my faculties of love; it was the usufruct of his irresistible strength that he bequeathed me. Imagine a Malte who, in the Paris that was so awful to him, might have had a lover, or even a friend! Should he ever have become so deeply confidential in things? For such things (he often told me in our few intimate conversations) to which you would bring the essence of life, first ask you: Are you free? Are you prepared to devote *all* your love to me, to lie with me as St. Julian the Hospitaler lay with the leper, bringing him the supreme embrace to which casual charity could never attain, but which is born of love, complete love, all the love that exists on Earth? And if the thing should see (this is how Malte put it to me) if the thing should see that you are otherwise involved, even with the barest iota of your attention, it will close in on itself; perhaps it may give you a word of recognition, throw you a vaguely friendly little sign (which is already a great deal for a human shut in amongst humans obsessed with misguided eloquence) . . . but it will refuse you its heart, to entrust you with its patient being, its sweet, sidereal constancy that makes it so similar to the constellations! For a thing to speak to you, you must keep it for a while as *the only thing that exists,* as the unique manifestation which, through the toil of your exclusive love, finds itself placed at the center of the universe and which, in that incomparable setting, is that very day waited upon by the angels.

What you read here, my sweet Friend, is a chapter from the lessons I received from Malte (my only friend through so many years of pain and temptation)—and I see that, unquestionably, you are saying the same thing, in speaking of your drawings and your paintings which seem worthy to you only in that amorous involvement with which brush or pen consummate the embrace, the voluptuous, caressing act of possession. The "sleeping woman" and a certain aspect of the "young girl at the red balcony in springtime," as well as the appearance of the other young girl in the tragic embrasure of the eternal window . . . gave me such palpitations of the heart, not only sensual, but *infinite,* you know the kind of heart palpitations that might be caused as well by a quickly run race as by the arrival of a lover or by that shock of well-being with which springtime influences attack us: it was a kind of emotion, *caused by all of these simultaneously* . . . I leave it to you to imagine its strength. That is, in fact, what I meant to say when I wrote you that what surprises me most in each pastel is the unity of feeling in which the object is every time contained; *a unique, tempestuous breath of feeling, a unique gesture of passion has, in one fell swoop, moved it close to the heart; it's a total manumission* . . . and still it is you, oh lover of Earth and sky, that I sing! Still the strength of your arms and the ineffable glory they take in their obedience to your sovereign heart, to your glorious heart, to your new and ancient heart, to your spring and summer heart, to your heart which, did it not contain that dazzling season of blossoms, would long ago have become a star, not so awfully great as Venus, but of the same flame, the same heavenly conflagration!

Dearest, hear me, I am glad of not leaving. Everything is beginning to close me in once more, and I must recapture the feeling that this reclusion is kind and beneficent and the fulfillment of my desires. When I left on the 22nd—the time up until then *was but a waiting period*, despite myself, *and the time since my return from Geneva until the Xs[4] arrival, also a kind of wait—so that until mid-January all is nothing but an aftereffect, an interruption*! And all my powers making their way to the

---

4. Anton Kippenberg, Rilke's publisher, and his wife Katharina.

---

inner centers will have to retrace their steps toward the exterior, continuously toward the *visible*. It is true that I have time—*months,* since in all probability the Xs won't return to Berg until May . . . but one never knows. The ill-fated years have left me with a kind of *Schreck-haftigkeit,* a constant apprehension of anything that might come along to destroy . . . Don't be frightened by the word "fate" which I used in my last letter; "fate" is what I call all the outside events (including illness, for example) which can inevitably come to disrupt and annihilate a temperament that is solitary by nature. Cézanne understood this well when, during the last thirty years of his life, he avoided anything that might "get its hooks into you," as he expressed it, and when, believer and devotee of tradition though he was, he nevertheless refused to attend his mother's funeral so as not to lose one day of work. Hearing of this was like being pierced with an arrow for me, but with a flaming arrow which, in piercing my heart, left it burning with clearsightedness. There are few artists these days who can conceive of such obstinacy, such violent stubborn-ness, but I believe that, without it, one remains at the outskirts of art, which in itself is yet rich enough to allow of some pleasant discoveries, but where one nev-ertheless participates merely as a gambler at the table who, while occasionally throwing a "good roll," remains ever subject to luck, which is but the dexterous tamed monkey of the law.

It was time for luncheon. I thought of your orders: I ate calmly, with the attention of a schoolboy pursuing a problem that finds solution in his mouth: a noodle soup, rice, carrots, and dessert, my coffee afterwards—and here I am once more. A light snow is falling, and in the very center of the sky above the fountain that is set off from the whiteness of the background by the reversal of its motion, at the very top, hangs a vaguely disc-shaped sun, without any rays or any strength, which in a moment will be swallowed up by the foggy atmosphere that struggles against this attempt at lighting. Already, looking up again, I see only a thin glow, similar to a spot on a piece of greyish paper that has been scratched with a penknife to remove an inkstain, at the same time working through the paper's thickness.

Beloved, do not misunderstand: all that I have just written you *is not to defend myself from your summons*— you yourself have consigned it to its perpetual inner state that requires no actual consummation for the moment; *it is from the summons I feel within myself, constantly calling me to you, that I defend myself.* I'll explain. I'm talking to myself in front of you—understand that, my Friend.

Oh, my very Dearest, reading the letter in which I speak of the torments of my childhood, you thought of "that afternoon" when, for the first time, I told you about that murderous time that assaulted me in my very tenderest youth, filling my soul with hurtful astonishment and a terror truly greater than life. "That afternoon . . ." I recall it often during my constitutionals in the park; again the other day, I saw it all, with that remembrance, both gentle and powerful, that perhaps overwhelmed the angel when he thought of that inexpressible moment when, trembling himself, he brought the piercing annunciation to the Virgin Mary. Oh! if only I could use the voice already within you, without it passing through my mouth, to tell you the story of our love, you would be washed in a flood of bliss . . . for it is far more beautiful than we can even imagine it; our memory, so swollen by the manifold harvest of this year of blessings, is yet insufficient to hold the entire crop: three quarters of which, you may be sure, remain outside, on the open wind . . .

That moment when you looked at me "as a virgin." Of a sudden, your face lost all expression, *all*, it renounced, it relinquished everything, all its complacencies, all its niceties, all its usual charms; it became quite somber, entirely empty for a fraction of a second . . . and in that new space, which was that of a moment of inception, was born, erupted, a new lucidity, oh, a lucidity whose description will forever be denied to man and angel, and which only a child could perceive in the morning air of his most innocent summer's day. *That I saw.* From that moment on, as to life, I can die. Seeing your face transfigured in love and entirely filled with that youth, that virginity that was preserved within you so as one day to dazzle me, I understood that the totality of splendors far surpasses the number of all hurts and all anguish that I have ever experienced. Do you understand? In thinking on this the other day, I recalled a line which long ago I wrote to Night, apostrophizing it:

Du Dunkel aus Licht[5]

Your lovely face was just that, overtaken by a new radiance in the middle of its dark transition: *from its deepest solemnity, which was that of youth, arose the resplendence of all life—all life.*

Of that moment as of many others, by the way, and even of some that were, so to speak, unapparent— *unscheinbar*—I do not understand how they managed to slip by! On several occasions since that event, we have been enwrapped not in time, but in a permanence exempt from all duration, from all corruption, a vital constancy, a pure existence.

I do not know, Merline, whether such words have ever been shared between lovers, but I engrave them on this page as if on granite, and I tremble in writing them.

Beloved, if ever you are overcome by any distress, any pain of body or soul, picture within yourself your own face, your holy virgin's face, the chosen maiden's face, for I know that you felt the transfiguration that shone from you, just as strongly as Saint Teresa felt the divine penetration in the flash of stigmatization.

I believe that the "Black Virgins," at the instant when they express their assent to the worshipper kneeling before the altar, his heart heavy with vows and offerings, I believe that at the instant of the awaited miracle they have that golden smile of a youth that rejoins them

5. "You darkness from light."

from the world's first age, that dark brightness that casts no shadow.

Oh Friend, the day has almost fled while I have written you; in an hour they will come to pick up the mail. I close here.

Goodbye, my Friend, goodbye,
Take care, Take care,
Love yourself
for

René

(*Thursday, about 4*)

Forgive me for sending this registered, and any disturbance it should cause you, but there are so many important things in these heartfelt pages . . . My Love . . .

Letter XV
Schloss Berg am Irchel
Canton of Zurich
Before Christmas, 1920

On the envelope:
To accompany the parcels sent yesterday.
Please do not read until Christmas night.

Oh my gentle Friend,

May the holiday be good to us, may it be blessed! May
the intensity of my ineffable presence allow you to forget the negligible absence which, at any moment, might
seem apparent if you look about you: but the room is
brimming with Christmas, brimming with those happy
preparations that take up so much of your time . . . And
if, confounded by the exterior world, you should take
refuge within yourself, is it possible that you should fail
even for an instant to recognize me there—I, who with
the violence of a hurricane and, at the same time, the
magic of an alchemist, have entered your heart and
filled your being—do you need any other proof that I

am within you, of that very sweetness with which you seem almost weakened? If at all possible, may you take even firmer possession of our treasures, of our true acquisitions, of our expanded horizons, of our broadened experience, of our swollen, magnified hearts—I believe it would so engross you that you would almost wish to postpone the given moment of our embrace—to first complete this new universe of the soul, and to become acquainted with this new consciousness with which your life has overflowed for months.

Oh Beloved, let us each do our own little share of work. That which we have been able to lavish on one another is limited neither to memories nor to promises; it is a new way of life, of sleep, of awakening, of staring out of the window, is it not?—well, my very Dearest, let us practice our very holy new religion independently, and may we have the patience humbly to discover, while it is not given us to celebrate them together, the sublime piety of our oneness and every law of our intimate emotion! Let us accept its greatest scope. If your soul opens itself to heaven's revelations as you might inhale a rose's perfume, if you draw into your life Venus' brilliance as once you used to enliven it with the little spark of glowing remorse, you accept dimension such that the spatial distance between our daily realities can no longer seem of any importance to you. Oh, and here again, as so often in these letters, I am speaking as much *for myself* as for you, because I too (as you have seen all too clearly these last weeks), have an anguished heart that calls for you, and which, when you are not there, sometimes suddenly stumbles and despairs. Even so, my Friend, I am proud and I am pleased to have found myself with the strength to remain despite all the violence of my desire, in the place allotted me this winter of renewal, and I would wish that, henceforth, instead of impoverishing and aggrieving it, this victory might enhance the glory of our Christmas holiday with something pure, something strong—in short, a limpidity to render it even more innocent and radiant.

Beloved, shall we feel it this way?

My thoughts are with you. I am deeply empathetic to your heart's condition, my Friend, solemn this day in the midst of the Nativity under the shadow of all those feelings that stem from the death of your revered father, the anniversary of which, falling this year as it does on a Friday, will be even more saliently felt. How lucky you are to be able to unite in the same splendor the miraculous birth of the Holy Infant and the mystery of the death of that blessed patriarch whose strength kindled the flame of your blazing life at your mother's breast. I would kneel before him, that he might give me, too, his benediction; may my encircling arms protect you as much as that old man's two hands which, descending from the heights of prayer, came to alight on your head.

May my tenderness be as worthy as that other priestly, parental tenderness—and may it grow as strong!

René

P.S. Happy, happy holiday. In the parcel: a few of my books, and another herewith. I have inscribed only our names as a dedication, since anybody might pick up these books—but you must read everything that I was unable to write in ink. Here and there, I have added notes so as to allow you a more personal appropriation of these already ancient works of mine—but which will speak to you nevertheless of that same René whom it has pleased God to make beloved of you . . .

Happy, happy holiday!

P.S. I am warning you now that I have sprouted an awful mendicant's goatee, bristling and disgusting—my barber in Paris, while politely shaving me, would always say: *"Monsieur* does not have a good beard"— and he was quite right, for it is growing without rhyme or reason, dazedly, like the beard of a blind man or a lapsed monk. For the time being I am letting it do so, for a barber is impossible to come by—even the one in Flaach, who also exercises the gentle profession of blacksmith, cannot come since the roads are closed— and in using the "Gillette" I only scratch myself up terribly; I end up removing one layer of skin after another and wasting a great deal of time in this desperate procedure. For this reason I am allowing myself to disappear beneath this hirsute mask for which L. seems to have forgiven me—or else, quite possibly, she has never actually looked at me.

Beloved, my dispatch to X. left yesterday, along with your drawing of B. and a long letter. I think that despite the slowness of the mail, it should arrive just in time for his holiday.

Please excuse me for writing the other day, in speaking of the arms that B. had painted on his buckler, "the thorny rose;" I noticed immediately afterwards that I should have said: "the rose with ear of corn . . ." it is a great wrong to misrepresent a knight's coat of arms. I am very sorry.

Letter XVI

Schloss Berg am Irchel
Canton of Zurich
Saturday, February 13, 1921

... My God, what a vacation atmosphere! Do you know, the only thing I feel capable of doing today is to go pick you up at Eglisau ... (It is so pleasant to recall that I did not see you get off the train ... You were there like a flower that had just bloomed, and it seems that I have only to go there to pick you.) The other Saturday when you were suddenly there, it felt as though it were New Year's Day ... Today I find that you absolutely should be here, because it feels like Easter. How will it all end, all these hallucinations of holidays one after another? It's awful. I have been walking; again yesterday I went all the way to Rheinau, an ancient Benedictine monastery located in a bend of the Rhine. I walked for five hours—and the steps I took, thousands of steps, alas, did not lead me into myself, like the hundred and twenty one that I used to take in the park. I am really walking outdoors, out amongst all the promising little birdsongs, alas, so compromising for me that I should listen to other voices and other whisperings. I returned here entirely changed—with a terrible need to flee myself, not to descend into myself, to travel . . . but it will all calm down, for the weather, too, will soon curb its premature enthusiasm, and we will take to the indoors.

. . . Oh my friend, how have the seasons intermingled, and this time not for us alone! I would like to draw the curtains and shut the doors and build up my winter obstinacy, despite everything, to summon concentration, my inner voices . . . Will I have the strength, the stubbornness . . .?

How I would have loved to take you in my arms after the departure on Wednesday, and to have you weep against me . . . Perhaps that would have cured my desiccation.

As I write all this, my entire being floats toward you . . . No, at this moment I am not here, I am there where you are . . .

I can understand why you don't like the city—but without going by rue du Puits-Saint-Pierre, take yourself sometimes to the bench behind the cathedral for a minute. Don't sit down, for that corner is still too cold this time of year—but revel in the shadow on the house opposite, God's own sundial revealing calm and peaceful weather.

Oh, today is a day for walking, is it not? How I should

like, in this merry sunshine, to go with you to market, to buy eggs and butter.

You are not going to alter the lining of the faithful little hat, are you? And send me, in centimeters, the height of the "adorable Page." (To share all my worries with you, I hope he does not come too close to reality, like the black knight in his time!)

Have a good Sunday, my beloved friend, enjoy a good meal. Do you take your meals in the kitchen? I ask so that I might sometimes sit myself next to you.

Yes, I will let you know when I am descending into my "mines," into the impenetrability of work; but in the meantime, speak to me still, oh! speak, sing, my friend,

René

(*Saturday noon*)

P.S. Luckily this letter hasn't been sealed. I have just received your golden dates, lovely on their bed of flowers. I was still thinking about them this morning! How good it is to understand one another, desire for desire, thought for thought. Oh my friend, what sunshine: it is you who are in the air.

René

Letter XVII
Wednesday, February 16, 1921

Infinite thanks for your two letters of Monday and
Tuesday, and for receiving my flowers with the other
half of that prodigious joy I felt in choosing them! Your
first letter, like a conductor's baton, had already given
the signal to my things that they could begin their con-
cert of serenity; each thing stood there waiting with its
instrument, but it is only now that they shall make their
music of silence. This time, your blessing has remained
pervasive—everything is beneficent and clear around
me—and in pure harmony.

And when I open the dresser drawer, your drawing
stares back at me and I bend over it like a sign from
heaven reflected in limpid waters.

The weather was splendid yesterday, and leaving the
lovely little post office in Flaach (where I spoke of you to

the old woman, describing the pleasure you had taken in her surroundings), I set off (at two o'clock) upon the road just across from the post office—I took a marvelous walk through fields and woods, quite buoyant, removing my coat and strolling for all the world the way a god might use a brand new human body that he is only to inhabit for a few hours and which he suffuses with his divine consciousness, experiencing all the while the benefits of this physical instrument. It was indescribably liberating. The countryside was beautiful, alluring; at every turn the road aroused such naive curiosity that one followed it like a promise forever renewed. I forded a little river (the "Thur") whose banks were of a charming russet brown that in the treetops seemed to fade to tan and lose itself in the golden tones of the encroaching atmosphere. Along this entire path I met not a soul. I was as if alone in the world and my heart was sufficient in itself to respond amply. Yet sometimes I stopped to call to you—and your absence had no density—and you came tenderly to permeate me; you looked through my eyes at what I showed you and I used your delicious pleasure as if it were my very own.

The clocktower of the Flaach church showed a quarter to six when I returned home!

The weather is quite different this morning, a stiff wind that appears to carry snow, but I had such a happy recollection of yesterday's outing that I took a brisk walk nevertheless, passing by Eigenthal castle—so as to pace myself by walking.

But here I am storytelling—when all I wanted was to say hello, my Beloved . . .

Congratulate B. for me, and tell him I am happy for his success. Each one of you makes me happy in your own way—how could I ever deserve it? I kiss you—can you feel it?

René

Letter XVIII
Thursday, February 17, 1921

Oh my Dearest,

What a gentle and miraculous communion in our Tuesday walks! I now understand the sense of well-being that I experienced on my walk, and how I could be so solitary and still find it so easy to summon you. As I told you, your absence had no density. It's because you too were walking beneath that same sun, with that same happy elation. Just think, Beloved: at one moment the fleeting idea came to me to compare our day in V. to my little extemporaneous excursion. It is not so much that the countryside reminded me of the other, but the air, the sunshine, my way of walking, an entirely innocent receptivity—in a word, the blessing I felt within myself—something inexpressible lent itself to that comparison . . . I understand now how much we belonged to one another, on the same heart's path, and that our smile was more ashine on the air than the sun itself. *Everything that happens to us, without our wanting or soliciting it, is it not always splendid and of the purest justice, like that feeling that impelled us both into the open air—that rejoicing—can anything be more sharing, more blissful?*

What you say about harmonizing color is delightful, my Friend; it reads like beautiful poetry. How I see you now in your letters . . . !

My pains and discomforts are entirely unimportant and deserve no special attention. The only pains that can alarm me are yours. You must avoid fatigue, and above all the humidity of the pre-springtime countryside.

I have just received a charming letter from G.S.,[1] very friendly and solicitous of my health and my solitude. Would you care perhaps to take a walk to Petit Saconnex on Thursday or Sunday afternoon?

I must run to Flaach. Farewell.

René

---

1. Guido von Salis owned a chalet in the hamlet of Petit Saconnex, on the outskirts of Geneva.

Letter XIX
Schloss Berg am Irchel
Canton of Zurich
February 20, 1921

Thank you, my Love, for coming to me again this Sunday. I read you last night, I reread you to start off my morning today, before giving myself to Moréas'[1] stanzas, which arrived here directly from Paris and which I am now comparing to Mr. Ungern-Sternberg's translations. That is how I have spent half of this Sunday, which will not pass without making me dream long and tenderly of that of eight days ago.

How well I saw you as I slept in the sunshine, Beloved. I believe it must be mutual, and that your

---

1. Yannis Papadiamantopoulos (1856–1910), pseudonym Jean Moréas. Greek poet, leading Symbolist after 1884, founder of the *école romane* in 1891.

---

canvas, once begun, set to painting you as you slept, so present and visible to me were you in your armchair! What you say about the flowers before you and about their background is more or less the concept for that lecture on Cézanne that I've thought of giving one day. It is so true . . . But having this sublime conception of painting, how can you hope, my gentle Beloved, that your arms and your head should suffice you in it? Don't forget that it was this task at which Cézanne's rabid male ego exhausted itself for thirty-five years of his life, and that to take but a few steps along this road of passion, he had to renounce everything, not with contempt but with the heroism of one who has chosen the lineaments of death out of love for life!

I nevertheless share P.'s[2] opinion that you are creating something very beautiful, so long as you persist slowly between two sleeps! For the moment, in your case I'm inclined to call it sleep rather than work, that regenerative sleep, that sweet sleep filled with abstractedness and abandon, similar to the one that held you when the "Stag" came to show you its enormous rack. *Be kind to this beneficent sleep;* never deny yourself to it. It is also a god, and so much my friend that I lend you to him without the slightest jealousy, being sure that he knows me through and through, and that if he speaks to you of me, it is without slander of any sort.

---

2. Merline's elder son, Pierre Klossowski, later a writer. Rilke was to be instrumental in persuading André Gide, amongst others, to fund Pierre's education in Paris.

Oh dearest, you may laugh at me without restraint if what I am about to tell you sounds superstitious . . . but never speak to me about the "Elegies" . . . I beg you! Yesterday's letter will have served to convince you that I am far, far from my work. I shall do my very utmost to draw nearer, but should I approach slowly through rigorous discipline exercised every day, even should I come near enough to touch it, I shall still—and for a long time—be far from that supreme effort. I can use no subterfuge, nor even the slightest straightforward attempt to penetrate that ineffable sphere that has never been accessible to me except after a period of total submission and daily obedience, primarily spent in carrying out orders of minor importance. It would no longer be my solitude were I to reveal all its laws to you—but I am permitted to confide that I have a long road ahead of me to reach the starting point . . .

My very Dearest, do not hold it against me that I reveal all this to you, without dissembling any of my perhaps exaggerated and perhaps (which would be worse) pedantic sensibility. The life of any man who has reached a certain level of his commitment to art undergoes mutilations that, in a certain sense, bring him to the brink of mania; such boldness is required in art, even if outside it the artist often exhibits a ridiculous pusillanimity; it's that his courage . . . (*I have preferred to describe it this way: "It may be true that I am a* hare-foot[3]—*but for all that I can also be the entire hare on occasion!" From the beginning, that has been my apology*

3. *Hasenfuss,* i.e., coward.

---

before God—and now here I am justifying myself to you, my Dear. You should reread what I once wrote you in that long letter about Malte—*ah, it's always the same thing! Are you reluctant to hear it? And yet, sitting before your flowers while they demand your entire soul much more than your delightful arms, you write me precisely the same thing!*)

Leni has gone out for the whole afternoon—you know the quiet—from the right the cock's crow reaches me borne on the capricious wind (at once I want to be within the cock to learn beneath which of his feathers he feels the next rain coming and whatever change of wind is in store).

Yesterday, at my request, Mr. T. sent me my Froissard [*sic*] and the Montaigne—I am very glad to own these two lovely editions, and at such a low price. Mr. T. tells me that, while remaining a secondhand bookseller, he is soon to become the publisher of a new review, and having vaguely discovered that I have a certain literary affiliation, invites me to collaborate "if I should feel so inclined." But it seems that "name-snatching" is secretly practiced in his store, for one gentleman who happened to be there while Mr. T. was wrapping my books confesses that he has fortuitously seen my name, and begs, rather offhandedly at that, the privilege of translating my *Cornet*,[4] in which he claims to be all "wrapped up." You understand that I must reject all such extraneous efforts of gratuitous kindness.

---

4. R. M. Rilke, *The Lay of the Love and Death of the Cornet Christoph Rilke*, 1906. In 1921, the *Cornet* was by far the most popular of Rilke's works.

Beloved, please read (*im Litterarischen Echo*) Dauthendey's[5] letter—not so much to examine the state of
his soul, which is difficult for us to understand, but
infinitely tragic (just think: in his Paradise of love,
where all conspired to make him forget ill-fated Europe,
he was consumed with nostalgia for his country that
had become a hell!), not so much for that, but so that
you might read his description of the Javanese dances,
particularly that of the king and his three concubines . . .
How beautiful it is! My God, why do people live their
lives with morals that pinch like a tight disguise and
prevent them from discovering their invisible soul, that
dancer amongst the stars!

René

5. Maximilian Dauthendey (1867–1918). German poet. The out-
break of war in 1914 had trapped Dauthendey in the Far East.

Letter XX
Monday, February 23, 1921

Your long letter has just this minute arrived, and the little flowers that Leni will do her very best to preserve, and still more of those magnificent dates!

Dearest, I knew that you would be somewhat carried away in reading H.'s[1] book; it was rather for Hausenstein than for Klee that I sent it to you. For this way of seeing is very spiritual and occasionally quite funny. Don't forget that he himself, in speaking of Klee's manner of creation, uses the word "*Verhangnis.*"[2]

There is no other way of understanding Klee, except that

1. Wilhelm Hausenstein, art historian, diplomat, and friend of Rilke. The book referred to is *Kairuan* (1921).

2. Fate.

his *"fate,"* these days, is suggested to many unbelievers, laid at their feet, *so to speak; whereas Klee is able to use the "fate" attributed to him in a very particular way. Namely, he makes it truly ineluctable to himself by every means, and a fate must be genuine if it can't be shaken off. What is so moving, after the subject itself falls away, is that these days music and graphic art should take one another reciprocally as* subjects—*this short-circuit of the arts behind Nature's back, and that of imagination itself, is for me the most unsettling of contemporary phenomena, although a liberating one: for beyond that it can really go no further. But now, in reading through Hausenstein's witty book, I discover an immense serenity in myself, and conceive how everything actually fits together for me. And immediately afterwards (in which, I fear, Klee can no longer take part) everything falls back into place.*

During the war years (in 1915 Klee brought me about sixty of his compositions—in color—and I was allowed to keep them for months; they ofttimes excited and occupied me, especially in that Kairouan,[3] *which I know, could still be felt in them)—during those years, I often seemed to share this exact same experience, this disappearance of the object (for this is a question of faith, of knowing to what extent we accept one—and, into the bargain, wish to express ourselves through it; broken men then find themselves best signified by crumbling ruins) . . . One needs the obstinacy of a city dweller (and Hausenstein is one) to dare to pretend that nothing exists*

3. Rilke had visited Kairouan (in Tunisia) in 1910.

74

any more. With your little primroses, I can begin afresh; truly, nothing hinders me from seeing all things inexhaustible and unconsumed. Whence shall Art spring, if not from the joy and the tension of infinite renewal?

Beloved, I read "the dream" such as you entrusted it to me, and I thank you for it. It's so curious—*in the realm of your dreams everything is permitted, for everything is divinatory, great and fateful.*

Have a happy holiday tomorrow. May all your room feel its presence from earliest morning!

René

P.S. Forgive my hurry—I broke off my transcriptions to speak with you a while, and now I must run to Flaach!

Letter XXI
Tuesday, February 22, 1921

My Love,

Trembling with emotion, just as you wrote it, I read your letter last night by my warm fireside, after returning from Zurich. My table was overflowing with letters, some pressing—I tried to read a few, but understood only yours, my Friend; I kept coming back to it; at midnight it was still before me . . .

No, I had never dared to "push on to Geneva," not even in thought, *despite all my impatience to be with you, despite all my longing . . . ! I see and know only too well—and feel every day—what is now at stake for me. This urge to go out into the open air, toward you, you who appear to me like those patches in the blue sky that open out onto what is beyond our feelings—this urge to go out, Beloved, is surely correct, but at this moment in time it is "temptation" all the same—precisely that temptation to which one must not suc-*

cumb when the time has come to give oneself entirely to the great fulfillments and achievements. You see, I cannot be mistaken (no matter how much I would wish to be!); my inner gaze is indescribably keen, even when my emotion lends its vibration to everything—my gaze looks beyond to another pure, oh so pure outline: I know that, since my return, I shall have to recapture my innermost order from the beginning, just like last November. . . .

You must not forget what these years have been for me and done to me with their interruptions—this "consciousness," which has become indispensable to me, is not some simple transition from receptivity to productivity, from distraction to concentration: it is the process of healing wounds, requiring infinite stasis and isolation and patience. It is only beyond the healing, which I am still far from having effected, that lies the beginning of achievement, of the new motion, supermotion, flight.

Beloved, have patience with me.

Life for me is not that ruler who, as you write, "has given me everything"—that doesn't sit right with me. I have out-guessed and foreknown many a thing it has not given me, and as for its way of "giving," as they say, it has greatly troubled me since childhood; where others seemed to receive "gifts," I received only burdens—simply because I understood well beforehand the spirit of such great gifts. Love behaved unreasonably with me, finally trying to force its alluring fruit into my delighted eye, as if the eye had been a mouth—yes, I can assure you that love gave me everything only when it was able to remain aloft without so much as perching one foot on my heart.

My Friend, I am not making any affirmations here that

should frighten you, for how many moments of sublime blitheness have there been between us, and what inexhaustible discovery did we make yet again just the other day, that unforgettable Sunday morning, here before my fireplace . . .

After all that I have experienced, all that I can wish is that fate should have no designs on us (we are not made of such cloth), but that, beyond its reach, we may allow ourselves the proof—which was always the nature of our mutual delight—of an almost heavenly exaltation, somewhere on the islands of space where the laws of gravity do not hold; let us never seek to examine the machinery *of our mutual rapture and of our elevation to our common God. Let the mystery we sense in* him remain His *alone, and never ours, so that we may suddenly seem to stand in this "real" world as if with something misappropriated that attracts people's attention.*

Allow me henceforth, Dearest, allow me during the coming months, while this refuge remains available to me, to order and clarify my life. (I could not survive much longer under these clouds that have lasted for years!) That is what matters to me, and not the Elegies at all, nor some nebulous productivity—I am not an "author" who "makes books." The Elegies themselves (or whatever it was that was once given me) were only the result of an inner constitution, an inner progress, of a purer and more extensive becoming[1] *of my entire interrupted and shaken nature. That is why I was so startled when you recently referred to the Elegies as a "work" —and why (oh forgive me!) I nearly reprimanded you.*

Understand me: so strongly do I belong to and serve my

---

1. *Reiner-Umfassender-gewordenseins.*

---

work—I cannot in any way draw it forth—which is why I was so moved by Bonsels'[2] *words, that* no extreme state can achieve more than that of "readiness"*—it is for "readiness" that I am currently struggling, so let no one come to touch or disturb me, for like the growth of crystal, readiness depends on the most distant influences that reach us when we stand within the constellation, unperturbed by chance, caprice, desire, or resistance! Oh, my dearest, believe me, I know "the world." I want nothing but to "remain within the law;" how could that possibly do you any harm? Shall we then hope for any lessons or comforts other than those that are based on that same law? Woe to the love that conflicts with the stars!*

At the moment I am powerless, like anyone who has allowed himself to be degraded under the daily influences of fatalities; the war years seem to have put me wrong—my entire existence has grown false in their twilight—I must put myself to rights once more:

Your love in certain hours has contributed infinitely to strengthen me—I spend whole days in gratitude to its scope and splendor, to which I owe my future. But decisions fall only on the being alone, *and I must yet again seize and replenish my own, and adjust it to the great connections to which I have aspired since childhood, oh so infinitely more than to any happiness!*

Aren't you aware that all is magnificent between us? Have two lovers ever experienced such reciprocity, with such expec-

2. Waldemar Bonsels, 1881–1952. German writer, author of *Menschenwege* (1918) and *Eros und die Evangelien* (1920). (Cf. Letter xxxvi.)

tation in their open arms, as if everything between them hitherto had been but anticipation of that which they had never yet seen, and all the evidence of their hearts had become the endless suspicion of that which they had so strongly felt already? Does this not speak well of us, Beloved, that we should have been able to maintain it, to leave it and retrieve it thus?

You are right: let us—as far as possible—let us consent to the summer, that it be ours, *in some quiet place. May we finally have a time to face each other and place our stamps on one another . . .*

I am writing in all haste. This letter may be full of mistakes—I have no time to reread it. Three business letters must be sent off with this one.

But I will write to you again this week, Beloved, will tell you before I set off for the isle of work.

Oh understand, feel and believe that in suffering, it is from bliss that you suffer.

René

Letter XXII

Schloss Berg am Irchel
March 7, 1921, Tuesday

Darling,

This little letter comes in place of one I had written you on Sunday and did not send; I brought it home with me from Flaach. It is before me now, tenderly reproaching you in a way you are familiar with, and essentially repeating things I have better expressed to you elsewhere; for that reason I deemed it useless.

It upsets me when, as in your last two letters, you speak to me of an "abyss of suffering" and of your "sadness." I should have liked to have been a sun powerful enough to dry up ... many tears as yet unshed, which you are brewing in some valley of your heart where it rains continuously.

I feel so selfish at the moment that I could wish, not to read that you are happy, but at least to receive some evidence of your tranquility, of your courage. Is that too much to ask of the strength of your love? Is it impossible for you to expend just a little of it to my benefit, and for you to be calm, to become a part and the buttress, so to speak, of that tranquility, of that poise which I have so long desired for myself and which (as you know) is the fundamental condition of my life here? But here I have come round yet again to repeating ideas you have long known, and if you write differently, it must surely be that you lack the strength to dominate your heart, and so I must resign myself, for you have spent so much—in strength—these past months . . . And yet with what joy do I greet the least glimmer in your letters—alas, but barely expressed before you extinguish it with your own hands. Why? Why? You write: "The other day I almost had the impulse to create something," and you hasten to add: "But I've lost it!" Beloved, speak to me, I beg you; let us discuss all the possibilities that seem feasible to you . . . It's heartbreaking to see you succumb to the idleness of a nocuous grief that does not even give rise to dreams. I would rest easy if I knew that you were taking your life upon yourself, as you did the whole time in G., with such marvelous energy; would you have me crushed beneath the weight of the suspicion that it was I who destroyed that youthful and, despite everything, joyous impulse? . . .

Oh, how I would bless the day that brought me better tidings of you, like those you sent me some ten days ago, after having received my letter which you claimed to have understood, and which seemed to have brought you back to yourself.

Allow me to suffer less for a while, my Friend: sustain

yourself, let happy memories bear you along, they are always there if your strength should fail you; and their current never reverses itself; even when passing through foggy lands, it flows toward the future! My God, if I could show you the smile you wore the other Monday, as we were saying our goodbyes on the train—it was rich enough to live on for three years!

I have begun rereading Keyserling's important Travel Diary,[1] *which from the very first page seizes the attention and demands the most intense participation. In one of the first chapters, during the crossing of the Indian Ocean, he notes: "When I do the work that I am compelled to do, my nervous system must be finely tuned, my attention uncluttered, my heart serene . . ." You see, the same goes for me; I am now able to give myself every possible thing—but this serene disposition must come to me from you, Dearest. Is it obstinacy, then, when again and again I imagine that you could be the guardian angel of these conditions, which your love is able to create so inexhaustibly, only so long as it shares in their results? Is it so very different to do the same for the silent, absent one, absorbed in himself?*

It is not for this reason, but for many others that are more significant for you, that I would wish you to read Keyserling's Diary, *to which you have hitherto been wholly unreceptive—it is the most "formative" book of our times, not in the sense that it is educational—but because it works upon us and within us: dissolving our dependencies, replacing them,*

---

1. Count Hermann Keyserling, 1880–1946. German philosopher, author of *Reisetagebuch eines Philosophen* (*Travel Diary of a Philosopher*) (1919).

---

almost exclusively, with relationships. This book firmly grasps the most free and receptive attitude to which a European mind can attain today—and if Hausenstein's book, as a liberation of things that have become perceptibly absent to us, was able to move you so deeply, so in this book would you accept with gratitude the survival of the persistent realities of the world.[2] *I have recently been sent the entire work, so that I can lend you the first volume that I had borrowed and once brought to your room. Wouldn't you like to give it a try? I won't send it if you'd rather not, especially since I have just drowned you with books—was there one amongst them that appealed not only to you, but to your communal readings?*

Today I must make a renunciation that weighs heavily on me: Hermann Keyserling is speaking tonight to the Hollingen Reading Circle, and into the bargain, the people with whom he is staying have specifically invited me to spend the last part of the evening with their illustrious guest. It was a real effort to say no—yet it had to be, since Berg, free from the slightest disruption, has finally won its cause. Count Keyserling does not allow his lectures to be published, believing that the spoken word should only be spoken—so the material loss is just as irretrievable as the personal meeting at Martini's.

As for my friend B., I was not so wrong, then, to advise him not to disappear into the "crack," since, as far as school goes, he was already there. Happily, it was discovered in time! I remain nonetheless convinced that

---

2. *Welthaftenvorhandenheit.*

"B. exists,"[3] only it may always be rather difficult to determine the place in which he exists!

I have some wonderful wallflowers on the dresser. Everything else remains just as you know it; that is to say, the desk has been here for some time (I am writing on it), pushed against the cupboards to the left without noticeably altering the corner that you love. (Since you do not get the *Journal de Genève,* I am including this article on the Pitoëffs in Paris—and ask you to return it the next time.)

And speak to me of this "impulse"—*it is essential.*

René

3. In his preface to *Mitsou,* Rilke had written:

'. . . I assure you that sometimes, at twilight, the neighbor's cat jumps over my body, ignoring me, or as though to prove to the stupefied material world that I do not exist.' But Baltusz's drawings will serve to convince the reader: 'I am. Baltusz exists. There are no cats.'
    —Quoted by Donald Prater (cf. Introduction).

Letter XXIII
Tuesday, about two o'clock

I am quite distraught, Beloved, for having written you that plaintive letter yesterday, since it crossed with the *wonderful letter* which I have just received, and which makes you so immediate that I can feel you, that I can hold you against me, and that your love washes over me and my room and the park. Everything is full, everything overflows with it, my Friend.

Forgive me. In all truth, I have no excuse, unless it were that your last two letters were *so dejected.* . . . But now that you yourself speak of everything, I understand you: you are "sustaining" yourself admirably. Oh Beloved, how I sense the life in you, never have I sensed life so whole as I do in you—and what glory: that life loves me . . .

Forgive, Beloved.

I do not have time to write more. But give me a little sign of forgiveness . . . When I receive "stiff" letters from you, *I will always wait out the next: the one which resolves the dissonances. Oh, how this one has resolved itself like weeping into tears of joy! How often I would love to save such tears for you, Beloved.*

Beloved, I am glad for you that the sun has returned: is it *quite warm* once again?

And hurry, hurry, send your pardon to

René

Letter XXIV
Saturday before Palm Sunday, 1921

Dearest,

It is raining, and everyone here is saying, "finally"—
even the birds; but what would you say, if you lost your
sunshine? . . . Yet, in fact, the rain was needed; it is
falling gently, tenderly, each drop a caress, almost a kiss.
And since the gardener has now discovered the flower
beds and borders, I seem to notice certain progress in my
park that the rain will enhance, so long as it remains
gentle and nourishing.

Dearest, the drawings I received on Thursday night
with your sweet letters were like flowers, and I am ready
to believe that those contours of your body open and
close at certain hours, just like the contours of flowers.
What tenderness, what sensual delight you manage to
express in these lines, which are seen, imagined, and felt,
a hundred times true, and which you draw like your

paraph, like the signature of your heart whose name, like the name of God, is too marvelous to be spoken.

Oh my Love, alas, I will be unable to fulfill your wish, either at Easter or later, for I deem—and have long deemed—the *Invitation au Voyage*[1] untranslatable. I do not know whether, in his magnificent translations, Stefan George[2] has tried to create a German version; if he was able to do it (we'll look into it one day) then it surely must be acceptable and the *only* one that can be made. Personally, I can't see a way; what could be done with those two lines alone which you quoted me the other day, to find equivalents worthy of them? Our expressions differ too much in their vocal values: to render *"calme"* we lack a word with an *a* in the middle, the *u* in our *"Ruh"* is neither long nor serene enough, a compound word formed from *Nacht* and *Thal* would be needed, might perhaps approximate *"calme."* And for *"volupté,"* all we have is that inflated word that implies a judgment, almost a censure—and for *"luxe"*—nothing . . . and *"beauté:" Schonheit* is so different; and it could never manage to recreate the lulling rhythm which is that of life entirely under the influence of a moon of love. And then, to sum it all up, right at the beginning one is compelled to use a stupid if inevitable rhyme, if one wants to rhyme at all:

1. By Charles Baudelaire.

2. Stefan George, 1868–1933. Lyric poet, considered in large part responsible for the revival of German poetry at the end of the nineteenth century.

Meine Schwester, mein Kind,
Denk, war uns das lind

(*It's enough to make you run away and never return, and yet it's inescapable.*)

The Water Fountain: *that remains to be considered. I was reading it recently, perhaps at the very moment that you were citing the poem.* It's very beautiful, but I am not convinced that it can be translated.

How well you read and understood Gorky's notes.[3] It took a Russian writing about another Russian to show you a great love that can admire without being forced to furnish evidence of a feeling that is unexplainable by its very nature; he's not afraid to pile up so many weaknesses before you, so many failings, so many contradictions of that great, that very great man, and despite everything one senses rising through it an admiration that never stops. Nothing more true, more right, has ever been written on Tolstoy. During the years I made my travels in Russia, I was not mature enough to be aware of my state of mind before him,[4] but reading Gorky, I was as if comforted, for my feeling, while naturally being less developed, was limited by the same contrasts. My God, his stubborn faults were so easily detected, and the energy, the obstinacy he put into

3. Maxim Gorky (1868–1936).

4. Rilke met Tolstoy twice, in 1899 and 1900, on his trips to Russia.

keeping these faults intact made him so readily detest
able. But suddenly, behind him, one saw the angel of his
faults that upheld them within him like a form of innocence. And then he himself, the sublime artist, before
forcing his dogged faults on the whole world, began by
suppressing his art, the eternal splendor of his heart, and
in this terrible sacrifice, all unwittingly, he had already
reached that state of poverty he wished to manifest by
leaving his home a few days before his death. . . .

(A half hour later)

. . . I have just received your letter—I've read both of
them—I don't have enough time to write you before
rushing off to Flaach, but neither does your letter
require an answer—I know—I know—I understand
you. It is the voice, the song of your heart which is yours
and which is eternal.

But according to what you told me in the letter I
received Thursday night, you still had hopes of staying
another month; if I understand you, it is quite unnecessary for you to be abandoning yourself to visions of our
goodbyes so soon.

I too, my Friend, must prevent myself at all costs from
imagining that that door may one day no longer be
yours. I believe that I have never loved a door as much
as that one, every fiber of its wood is fragrant to me and
every vibration of my three knocks must be bouncing
through it still . . . and you can't take it with you!

Yes, it would be something else altogether if we were

to go abroad—it makes me shiver too. Mme. Z.[5] has just told me that tenants might come to see the castle one of these days ... Just think, if they should like it they might move in quite soon, and then I too would find myself in more or less the same situation of having to leave in haste and in the same uncertainty of my future home ...

But I am not thinking about it, I am currently distancing—anything that might destroy my painstaking concentration—for the worst would be to leave here having completed nothing. Thus, without looking any further, I continue to take each day granted me here to transform it into something that has inner durability, that is worth its weight in life and posterity. But how soon I need to have a ''home,'' serene like my fair Berg, but no longer threatened by such or such a stipulation ... If I were able to rent Berg, and to remain here a year longer, and you could come here later to spend your vacations—and mine! How different would be my life, my thoughts ... Beloved, have a good Sunday anyway! And even should the sky remain gray and overcast, have a good Sunday despite everything.

René

5. Lily Ziegler. She and her husband Richard owned Berg.

Letter XXV
Monday morning, March 21, 1921

Merline, my Beloved,

How I love that note you wrote, as if under dictation from the blackbird's first song—*it is like a blissful sheet of music that I should like to present to a blackbird, so that he might take up the entire piece, singing note by note.* But according to all the letters you send me, the season must be much more advanced over there. I can see you at the kitchen window, spying out the yellow buds of the chestnut tree, and when you showed me *die gespreizten Finger*[1]: the white and tender places which the sun had not kissed—I saw them as well, and I did what the sun had been unable to do, and I felt proud to be more privileged and ubiquitous than the god himself!

1. "Your fingers spread."

Yesterday, a rainy Sunday, as one might have fore-seen. In the afternoon a sort of storm which I welcomed with a certain satisfaction, for it made me feel *more secret, more real, more intimate within myself: we had experienced nothing like it for so long; the life seen outside the window is so different, splendid; but I, within whom there is so much to retrieve, will again need to stay covered over a long, long time, as the earth must be by the snow, when it achieves and imagines much more than in the time of its appearance and productivity. Toward the evening a fire burned in the fireplace and I became absorbed in my reading, much against my will (for reading, too, is restricted for me, and going to bed early, when I am not snowed under with work, is* de rigueur) *with the curiosity of a young girl in Funck-Brentano's detailed account of* L'Histoire du collier[2] (Marie-Antoinette, Cardinal Rohan, Jeanne de Valois de la Motte, etc.) *and the rich documentation gathered by Funck-Brentano made these people come so alive for me that I simply could not break away and go to sleep. Later, when I nevertheless managed to tear myself away and I had extinguished the candles, the night outside was full of shredded clouds, a moon running in the west whose beams through the clouds formed a luminous background behind the large pine to the right. The entire scene filled with the violent splashing of the fountain, which had not yet calmed down since the afternoon's storm and which fell with singular frequency in places where it does not normally fall. . . .*

2. Franz Funck-Brentano, 1862–1948. French historian. The book referred to is actually entitled *L'Affaire du collier* (1901).

Beloved,

How beautiful, what you wrote me in your last letter: *I keep thinking that if you really understand my life as you felt it then, it will remain rich and fulfilling in a way wholly different from how you ever imagined. These are certainly the most profound words you have ever written me, the greatest; how much space, freedom and happiness they give me! You see, the fear of your departure had not entered my heart such that it could interrupt me. If it must be so, so should you see nothing but the direction of the future, and the frame which it frankly offers you.*

Concerning what you say, my love, quoting a painful remark by R.S., I will personally answer you one day— oh my Friend, my life is so different! *Think that my life is neither formed nor influenced by family surroundings, I do not disappear into a certain other atmosphere that would make any demands on me and gorge me on indeterminate influences—I live nowhere but in the* world, *in that of the stars and the open wind—how could alienations exist in* this *one! The only thing [necessary] is that you should never see my work as a rival, and that, in what* it *demands of me, you should recognize the law to which we are all subject, even more so in that we are more intense of heart. But since your heart achieves its greatest and most glorious intensity in all that concerns us, how could my work not always seem pure and transparent to you—like something which by its very nature not only does not separate, but on the contrary brings us together.*

Shortly after your recent departure from Berg, a joyous departure, I wrote down for you, Beloved, who in reality was your only rival for me, if ever you had one . . . Oh, I'm not going to reveal it to you today! (That's the response to the fig tree episode!)

Beloved, to close:

Do as you like with the two paintings for Countess D.[3] Of course, it is not necessary for you to leave them "as security" with me. Do as you see fit; I think they will rather arrange for you to do a nice portrait of T., either in Nyon, or at Pottenstein, in Mme. D.'s wonderful castle, at a time when I too will be there. For I have long hoped to go there, where the countess has very kindly offered me quite a lovely apartment, peaceful and convenient, even for work! I have had no further news of the countess since she left; she promised to write me as soon as she knows her permanent address in England. I imagine that only then will it be decided *if* and *when* she is to return to Nyon, this year . . .

As for your books, return to me those you are not using and don't want! The Keyserling is not mine, as you know, and I'd also like to have the Gorky notes— but please, *before you leave!* as I have promised them to Comtessina V.[4] Prince H.[5] writes me at length concerning the Gorky fragments, which made a deep impression on him. (The prince knows Russia in depth. He owned vast lands there through his mother, and for a while, many years ago, there was some question of his

3. Mary Dobržensky.

4. Agapia Valmarana.

5. Alexander zu Hohenlohe, a pacifist known as the "Red Prince" for his political views.

having to become a Russian citizen, for according to the law it was the only means of keeping his properties, which otherwise should have been sold.)

Dear, sweet Friend, Merline! Sunshine! It's determined to push through! Over there as well? I wrote yesterday to M. de U., so I can return the Moréas to you, which I will do tomorrow, for perhaps you might like to go on with it occasionally.

And you are on holiday!

Goodbye, my Friend!

René

Behold, Beloved,

Almost despite myself I have made myself M. de U.'s rival. . . . I have translated three of Moréas' poems, which I am sending you along with his wonderful book. But I did it only for you and me, it will remain within our intimacy so as not to wrong its legitimate translator. In any case, two of these poems he had deemed untranslatable (*Relève-toi, mon âme et redeviens la cible*, p. 97, and *Coupez le myrte blanc aux bocages d'Athènes*, p. 133) and the third is the one whose translation I found unsuccessful because, for the line which I have already quoted you, he found an image that seemed weak and insipid to me, in comparison with the marvelously austere original.

What pride, what disdain in these poems, don't you think, what independence of rhythm which, at every step, seems to express ultimate decisions in its very bearing. Ah! How I wish I could read them to you.

I spent all of yesterday afternoon in front of the house, in the sunshine, rereading a hundred times the translations I had just done, and which seemed to me to possess an equally proud and haughtily decisive gait to them.

Read them, and tell me if you agree.

It's wonderful how, in these last years, the resources of French poetry have drawn it closer to ours; never before has it been so easy to translate.

By the way, Merline, you shouldn't say anything against rhyme. It is a very great goddess, the divinity of most secret and most ancient coincidences, and we should never allow her altar flame to be extinguished. She is very capricious; she can be neither foreseen nor summoned; she arrives like happiness, her hands full of gaily blossoming achievement.

If Vildrac,[1] for example, hardly uses rhyme, it is because he does not have the goddess' blessing and, being a true poet, he does not seek that which heaven has not granted him. In recompense, a rhyme sometimes passes his way and, in his simplicity, he has the sublime tact to pretend he hasn't even noticed it, so as not to compromise the freedom of that foreign goddess.

Behold the marvelous strength of Moréas' rhyme, for instance: evoked yet never sought, by its mysterious

---

1. Charles Messager, 1882–1971. Pseudonym Vildrac. French writer, co-founder with Georges Duhamel of the group L'Abbaye.

consent it lends a composure, a confidence, which nothing could replace. True rhyme is not a poetic device; it is a perpetually affirmative "yes" which the gods condescend to oppose to our most innocent emotions . . .

I close, my beautiful Friend—for I still have two letters to write before the two o'clock post.

René

(It is well, Beloved, that I am sending you the *Stances*,[2] that will spare me from the temptation of going on . . . What brightness again, what a summer sky, what sunshine! It feels as if all this were *you* . . .)

2. *Stances* (1889–1905), by Jean Moréas.

Letter XXVII
Schloss Berg am Irchel
Canton of Zurich
Thursday, March 24, 1921

Merline,

Every moment I wish I could fly to you, and ask you, "Oh, Beloved, do you feel this sunshine?" Where are you at this very instant? It's Thursday, almost four o'clock in the afternoon. Are you on your sofa? Oh! How I wish I could be with you!

Yesterday as I was about to leave for the post office, I found a yellow butterfly in my room, beating itself against the windowpane. I opened the window and gently urged it onto my finger, which I held outside in the hot, sunny air—but it didn't want to leave, it was quite content on my finger—just like that other one, the little blue butterfly in the Villette meadow, that was so happy to have found me. It evoked our whole walk for me. . . .

My Easter wishes? Cherished Friend, I wish that for a few days you might forget the uncertainties that threaten you so closely, so that you can be the cheerful companion of the moment, of revitalizing nature, of life, which loves you and which you adore in turn.

This is what I wish for you, gentle Friend . . . Make your days pleasant ones. You see, worries, too, must remain fresh; you mustn't abuse them by keeping them constantly in sight; that won't make them go away— *well-worn worries are the most durable.* And then you must hope, and then you must believe, and then you must love. With all of that, can you possibly have any time left for constant worrying? Surely not!

I wanted to write to you tomorrow—but it's Good Friday, and I've only just learned that the Flaach post office will only be open between ten and eleven, and I'm not sure I'll be able to get away at that hour. . . .

What I do send you, Beloved: the very night that I received the letter in which you spoke of your desire to have a translation of *L'Invitation au voyage,* I had just finished that other translation[1] for you, in which you will recognize our common preoccupation and reading of an afternoon at Berg—the most lovely afternoon we have spent here. It gave me such joy to feel that it could be done, that I did it all in one sitting, well, actually two, but quickly, and with a joyous sense of being carried

---

1. *Le Cimetière marin,* by Paul Valéry, 1871–1945, French Symbolist poet and philosopher.

---

away that reminded me of the same feeling that impels me into your arms!

Read it then, my Love, and may it be sweet and magnificent for your Easter heart! I must run to Flaach again this evening; one can feel, anticipate already the coolness of night.

And write me a line or two.

René

Letter XXVIII
Saturday before Easter
March 26, 1921

My Beloved,

Though I have only just arranged these little flowers—cut this morning in the park—in their nest, like a jeweler preparing a queen's finery, I cannot guarantee that they will arrive hearty enough to prolong their little interrupted lives in one of your little vases, between your hands, beneath the stronger sunshine of your gaze . . . Therefore, if you receive them withered, see in them my offering to your Easter heart, and may they at least transmit to you the memory they each contain: having seen me on my knees, tenderly cutting them, and not doing them the least bit of harm.

Yesterday was yet another day of infinite, inexhaustible splendor. . . .

The Colonel[1] was here, a little longer than on his last visit; we spent the whole morning together. He's done everything he can to rent Berg, not just for the summer as I had believed, but for several years. I find this comforting, for it will be all the more difficult to find a tenant for such a long lease. If it's nearly impossible to bring someone in for the fair season, it will be much more unlikely to come across people who will be willing to settle in for the entire year, most folk being stuck in the city at their work during that time—or at least compelled to seek somewhere more accessible.

With all this, the danger of my being evicted is less threatening and in any case not so imminent. And if by then it is impossible to rent, the Zs will be coming very late, so that I may be able to await the beginning of the summer here, having had the entire spring . . . Which would be perfect for all that I have in mind, because such inner preoccupation naturally suffers from the approach of any precisely defined *term*, even when it is still far off. Monsieur Z., who is very fond of Berg, was well pleased with his inspection of the park, the farm, etc. He was enchanted by my room, which gave off a holiday atmosphere simply because of the sun and of my joy of living in it, which lends all the objects a little smile that he had never seen in them before. I had flowers out, and everything presented itself in a manner such that he gazed upon his own house with a lover's eyes. In any case, it is well deserved. He talked a great

1. Richard Ziegler.

deal about his travels—he was arriving from Paris, which he found delightful—ah, my God, from *his* point of view . . . How much more is Paris, seen from the heights of the tower that is my heart, or glimpsed from the flowering valley that is yours!

Despite the holiday yesterday, I imagine you will have received the translations of Valéry. Are you happy with them, my very Dearest? The trouble is, in copying *L'Amateur de poèmes* a bit hastily (since the parcel had to go out earlier than I had counted on sending it), I allowed myself to be seduced into putting a word into it that bothers me terribly: please *cross it out,* Merline—it's that *"tadellos"*[2] (a word that was once fairly distinguished, but too disfigured by its abuse in everyday speech)—and replace it with *"rein"* (which I had originally used) *"in prachtvollen oder reinen Gruppen."*[3] Do so without fail, my Friend, for the knowledge that this *"tadellos"* is strutting about in the poem bothers me like a wisp of straw in the eye . . .

There we are, and again, a happy Sunday, but I leave it to my flowers to tell you the rest, *all of it.*

René

2. Splendid.

3. "In groups magnificent or pure."

Letter XXIX

Saturday after Easter, 1921

My dear Friend,

Flowers to my right, in front of me as well, on the window ledge, too, flowers on the desk, on the table behind me, on the stool by the sofa, and all alone, on the mantelpiece, *your red rose* . . .

Do you think the Madonna was stronger than my room, than *Berg*? Seeing her the first day, everything disappeared for me, and I saw as the only reality your little writing desk with all the objects that are upon it— in a word, everything that surrounded the locket, really; it was not yet here, no matter where I imagined it— there was always the little desk beneath it and that whole corner of your room blossomed around it . . . Little by little, all of this faded, and by yesterday the Madonna had become for me a sort of proof of the opposite—I understood that, since she *was able* to be here, your dear room will be no more within a few days. It's too painful to think about, Beloved . . . The locket is so beautiful against the black slate of my writing table—see it? Before me to the right, more or less in front of the framed calendar. And what you placed inside it . . . I have added the tenderest of kisses, and I lay on its sweet, scented lock the little ivory miniature which you had sent to me in Zurich in September. Yes, Friend, I will never be separated from this locket, it will accompany me everywhere.

And your notebook of the six little Remembrances, how it connects Berg to the rue P.J.

This sunshine! The espaliers are in bloom, apricots and peaches, the bumblebees and wasps are gathering their pollen, amongst the butterflies madly abandoning themselves to their enchanted game . . . *On Easter Sunday the weather was very changeable, but yesterday the sun was again triumphant, the afternoon and evening of a sublime clarity, and the night such that the clarity seemed forever affixed to the depths of heaven with great silver nails.*

Saturday I brought your Easter egg to the post office; little Walter was not there. He sought me out later beneath the hedgerows, *and without looking at me recited a sober speech, like a village mayor receiving his sovereign, expressing his thanks and his express duty to the lady who had graced him so surprisingly.* Speaking of hedgerows, I must describe a phenomenon to you. While picking some little flowers for you on Saturday morning, I noticed a drop of very sparkling water on a branch amongst the hedges. I felt the temptation to take it upon my finger, to drink this morning dew, a sweet and humble communion with nature—on the tongue, the drop possessed the slightly hollow limpidity it expressed to the eyes—but imagine this: in the afternoon, I see another drop just like that one in the same place, again I take it up . . . and it was bitter and salty like a real tear. . . . Oh, Beloved, have you been crying in my hedgerows?

The wise men here predict a week of snow at the beginning of April, which would not be so bad and may even be beneficial, if the nights aren't too bright, to moisten the terribly dry soil. I have not been able to keep busy on these two days of rest as I should have liked; I felt a little indisposed and chilled, and I expected it to end in a heavy spring cold . . . but nothing came of it.

Leni has made some very beautiful Easter eggs (which are at my left), blues, reds, and yellows, the latter dyed with herbs, gramineals whose little flowers and tiny foliage are perfectly imprinted; and a few violets have even left some of their color on them, a dark and naive blue-green.

I have been interrupted, Beloved, by the arrival of the mail! For our post offices having been closed yesterday, it is only now that I am receiving your little ''greeting for Easter Monday,'' the delightful and vibrant causerie of your heart that does really envelop me as you had wished, like a little breeze fluttering with tenderness.

You already know that your flowers arrived wonderfully well, that they are surrounding me, that they love me, and that they are thriving marvelously.

Oh, I can understand, dearest, why everyone is setting up a fuss over losing you from Geneva . . . It's not that they are only now becoming aware of it—but therein lies the laziness of life, when we don't always express all our delight and all our emotion. Furthermore, there are some who have always done so, such as, for instance, your bakerwoman!

Beloved, a quick glance: a letter from Breslau, a Mr. Carl Behr sends me a poem. A letter from La Landowska,[1] who writes that you described very well my yearning for work to her, that she doesn't wish to disturb me, that she will be in Paris around April 12th, and that she will take care of all my affairs from there.

I spent hours and hours on Sunday finally putting your letters in order—just those from the month of February are a distinct little treasure. I reread many of them, with pain, pity, with an inexpressible joy and, towards the end, with the ineffable desire to hold you in my arms, my Friend, whose heart spoke and resonated in those papers scattered about me.

Beloved, oh yes, it comes to me—that *everywhere* the doorbell can be rung three times, *our* three rings; the main thing is that you bring with you the heart in which they had such resonance.

I kiss you, Dearest.

René

1. Wanda Landowska, harpsichordist, whom Rilke had known in Paris.

Letter XXX
Saturday morning

Oh you most dear of dears,

Sun, strong and clear east wind, like a broadshouldered, purebrowed God he came to me on my morning walk. At the edge of the beeches, dandelions of astounding size have bloomed, to the joy of the bumblebees in search of work—ah! how can one avoid thinking of it—if we climbed together towards the woods—perhaps we would barely hear the ten thousand birds—ah, what would we hear, what would we hear, what would we know, my most Beautiful One, but us! us! and within us the world . . .

And all night the frogs in the swamp played their flutes of love, so confident, sometimes in three parts, the sublime harmony, in the beatitude of their easy loves and (I believe) without jealousy. And yet, a song as melancholy as if they had guessed that, with all this in their hearts, much more could have been made of it if they had not by chance been trapped in that old house-maid's purse that is a frog's body.

My love, your letter written after our telephone conversation—I picked it up myself yesterday evening, around six, in Flaach, whence I had to send an important piece of mail—and I read it, making a detour over the fields, again and again in the vast, rarified evening. Oh, Beloved, you too were shattered by our conversation! This "voice-to-voice," oh my Beloved, was very imprudent *of us, together we have* reopened a deep wound of yearning! *But that is just what I had foreseen when I recently warned you and begged you not to telephone from Zurich as you had planned, when you were passing through. This being near and remaining unattainable, who could bear it—it shook me like a storm, Beloved. And you, too, were staggered by it, poor children that we were before the great God. And my situation was far worse. Scarcely had I recovered and stabilized myself a little, when at noon yesterday the violence of your letter broke over me and shattered the entire young forest of my resistance. What devastation!*

My dear sweet child, let us now be proud and upright. Now consider that which is yours. Your letter—had two faces, one a little calmer, the other entirely turned towards departure—Dearest, I understand it, I foresaw it, and I was afraid that you might hesitate amongst these uncertainties—but that is the worst thing you could do. Better to make a decision no matter what!

Merline, my dear Friend, reflect *serenely* (*dies betonend*) upon all this. And do not write to people when you are agitated! You list so many letters written the day before yesterday. Learn this: one should never write in such moments when one feels overwhelmed and hemmed in on all sides; *these are moments ready made for keeping quiet!* For not only is it very helpful to one's inner concentration, which alone can offer some assistance in uncertainty, but it also spares one the pain of receiving equally confused answers. For nothing is harder than answering a letter written by a person in a muddle. One answers badly, and then there is the additional complication that when you receive the answer you are in an entirely different state of mind and in that alone, the letter, even if it was well written and thought out, will be of no use to you, *because urgent and decisive questions cannot be usefully discussed in letters sent more than a day's journey. One should express oneself in letters only during certain* average *moments, and not in moments of* extremity, *when at best only a spoken answer or an immediate influence can have any effect!*

I was waiting for the mail; nothing from you . . .

I kiss you, my sweet Friend. Have a loving Sunday.

René

Letter XXXI
Tuesday morning

Thank God, my Love, you are well. Last night I was *so* anxious for your letter that I went to Flaach at six o'clock to receive it an hour earlier. And you had that lovely Saturday, harmonious and clear—no, I think it marvelous that your room is once again graced with eight engravings. You see how you are loved—oh, I wish that my love, strong enough to create constellations around you, were there for something. I'd love to believe that you found those pictures because you were happy, and that I had made you so, my sweet, sweet Friend . . .

I had always thought that it was the poet's gift to make people see more clearly and more visually what it is they have, just by being with them, but you unconsciously went and did this good deed for Mme. S.; you too possess the faculty to make resplendent the pure and intimate joy of things which are sometimes invisible to those who see them on a daily basis. Is it the gift of the artist, who in the end is the only one who can see, *or is it the gift of those who are full of yearning?*

The spring, a house such as this—you say that it is drawn upon the air! *Ah, nothing must be missing, not even the old grey wall that surrounds the garden.*

Oh, that you had such a free, such a hopeful, such a magnanimous day! How it resounds for me when I touch it, how vibrant still is its metal from your light morning excursion, all that was in that day: to be beautiful, your own beauty, joy—your own joy—the silent woman whom you cheered and blessed in what is hers, the fair child that you painted, your work, your happiness, your hands, your heart beating, living, looking only within itself, turning outward only so as restlessly to seize the perceptible landscape, which never ceased passing through you, and you, perceiving it, were but perceiving the creativity and distances and abundance of your own nature. Was it not so, Dearest? Oh, I feel as if with eyes closed I were pressed against you, and you were our sight and our knowledge, and that you transformed everything outside into one spiritual inner being, and that you slipped it in as a vision beneath my eyelids.

Has the weather also changed over there? It was so set in its immutable clarity that a great, heaven-sent anger was needed to overthrow its constancy. When I went to get your letter last night, storms were brewing on every side, and the young meadows in their light green, which hitherto had known only clemency from the sky, were quite pale with fear in seeing the sumptuousness of its exaggerated, pathetic wrath—*but earlier, throughout the whole afternoon, the birds' cries were already like those of the summer, before the rain: isolated, more serious, more sonorous, each cry louder, as if a new aural measure had suddenly been adopted for hearing it. In the morning I heard the first oriole throwing out its "Vogel-Bülow" in its carefree, spendthrift's voice.*

. . . Good day, Beloved. I am contemplating the great buds of the chestnut trees beneath a grey sky that relaxes the eyes.

René

Letter XXXII
Schloss Berg am Irchel
Canton of Zurich
April 8, Friday

My dear, my tender Friend,

I am quite astonished to be writing you yet another Saturday; yesterday I was imagining you already on your way, but it is not until Sunday that you are leaving and I see that the route through Basel is much shorter and more direct. I am happy, Beloved, at your calm, serene decision, which is now above circumstance, and I admire your inventive activeness: that you were able to finish the portrait of the little boy . . .

As for me, I am making an effort at the moment not to consider the future and its vague anxieties; in any case, it would only deprive me of my "present" at Berg—which, by the way, has received a severe shock by an altogether unexpected disturbance, a disturbance which for the past two days has irritated and exasperated me.

Just imagine, an "electric sawmill" has been installed directly opposite, at the right exit to the park; it has been going since Tuesday and makes a continuous, atrocious racket of singing steel as with a dentist's cruelty it attacks that poor, wonderful timber brought down from the Irchel forest. My nerves are not very resistant at the moment, and I am suffering awfully from this intrusive obstacle, which I shall have to fight every day with a portion of my strength that I would so have wished to concentrate upon a single goal. I see furthermore that, as to this, my sensitivity is not exaggerated, for Leni, despite her peasant's constitution, complains of it too and sympathizes with my despair. If the windows are kept *tightly* shut, and if the wind is not blowing from that direction, it is relatively quiet, but all my walks in the park have become henceforward impossible. My beautiful silence! *Where are the days when I could write, the lovely fountain beating the measure of all the sounds here? This destruction of pure hearing is all the more devastating in that each thought only becomes real for me when I am also able to imagine it in tonal equivalencies, projecting it upon a background of purest hearing; to find my hearing so overcrowded with alien sounds is exactly as if I had to write on paper completely covered in scribbles and stains.* Forgive me for writing you so much, but it has rather overwhelmed me, my beautiful silence; again Saturday and Sunday I gave much thought to the fact that, if nothing else succeeds, at least I would have that for a few tranquil months, that wonderful silence of which the fall of the fountain seemed almost the very fabric, and which was now and then embroidered by the little bird calls and the melancholia of the frogs . . .

Not only for *my* use (very particular, if you will), but for anyone else as well, Berg has lost, through this ill-omened mechanical contraption, its principal attraction—for even if one is not thinking of intense work, even a person who simply wants to stroll through the park, read there in the summer . . . will be stripped of all pleasure by that continuous insinuation which undermines all attentiveness and which, I am certain, irritates nerves far less susceptible than mine. Oh well, enough—it's a bad sign! The railroad has not come to Berg—but through this industry the "times," our times, have imposed themselves on Berg, to remove the sense of tradition, hitherto intact, from this little manor. No, it's enough to make you cry. *And the awful machine "can do"; today it woke me at five o'clock in the morning—like children to whom one has given a trumpet, these madmen blow and blow from five A.M. to a quarter to eight in the evening; scarcely do these devils take the time to eat. Yes, it's the devil who has played this trick on me, or could it be the Providence of the good Lord, who wanted to make my departure from Berg less painful? Decidedly, He could not in His omniscience have found a better way—only, general and vague as He is, He started things too early. (What are one or two months in His reckoning! From His perspective, it more or less synchronized the onset of the sawmill with my clearing out! Oh precision, where are you?)*

In any case, the die was cast yesterday: Berg has been rented! The Colonel came with the tenants, and henceforth I

*know my "successor . . ." As to when they will move in,
there was no explicit discussion of it—it seems that I still have
about eight weeks. But I asked Z. to inform me the moment a
date has been set.* There you have it: everything turns,
turns, and approaches its end. *In the long run, what will
my good, sheltering, propitious Berg have been, including
Leni; what will it have been for me? What more can I wring
from it?* I will do my best against all odds!

The letter you wrote yesterday has just been brought
to me, my tender Friend—so our apartments were visited at *almost the same time.* Z. was here yesterday at two
o'clock with the new tenants. The sawmill was not
working at that moment; they too will be most disap-
pointed, *dieser kunftige Herr Schmidt*—I think that's his
name—when they notice the "illustrated"[1] silence.
Thank you, Dearest, for your kind, strong letter, overflowing with a love that anticipates everything with
patience and justice, despite what you call your
"volcanic temperament." I imagine your *adieus* to
Geneva, I am with you wherever you have yet to go,
and I am working in your heart with each "blow of
memory."

How lovely has that city been to us, how sparkling,
generous—and your room, where all my thoughts come
to rest—I cannot express what it has been to us . . . *I*

---

1. Rilke is making fun of "the future" Herr Schmidt's command
of French: Herr Schmidt has evidently referred to the *"silence illustré"*
("illustrated silence") when clearly he meant *"silence illustre"*
("illustrious silence").

believe that the moment you leave, the gods will transfigure your room amongst the stars, Beloved, and we will occasionally raise our eyes to it . . . It will be a beautiful new star revolving around Venus.

René

Letter XXXIII
Berg am Irchel Castle
Canton of Zurich
May 10, 1921,
about four o'clock in the afternoon

Dearest,

Without my explaining it to you (which in any case would be too painful an effort) you will understand what I am going through during these last days at Berg.

It is today (at six in the evening, like the other Sunday!) that I am leaving for Zurich. Boxes and trunks are packed—and despite everything, the large room still seems familiar, inviting, as if I were just beginning. And in truth, that's what I wish: that it were November 12 (last), and that I could shut myself away here . . .

Never have I left a place with such gratitude and such bitter regrets.

This is the last I am writing at *my* table.

I interrupt myself at length to stare out at the park, all clad in green, Dearest, so beautiful, so promising. At this moment the fountain is being whipped by a strong gale blowing out of the west, which causes a rapid change from too vivid sunshine to pattering rain that falls past the window like a sign of the times.

And I stare, I stare . . .

In a few days I will have regained my composure and I will write you with a little more good sense about what I plan to do at first and then later. Today it is the great farewells that occupy my entire heart. Oh understand, my Friend, understand and forgive me this sadness and this weakness.

René

While I am still unable to provide a new address, that of Berg will remain valid; everything will be forwarded.

I think I may remain in Switzerland for three or four weeks—and, if at all possible, *not* in Zurich! *Where?* I still haven't the faintest idea!

Letter XXXIV
Le Prieuré d'Étoy
Canton of Vaud, Switzerland
May 26, 1921, Thursday

My dear Friend,

I have just received your three letters, written in such different states of mind, but all three born of your suffering, my poor friend. It is for me to beg your forgiveness for having spoken yet again of this winter—alas, it was necessary, to bring you "up-to-date," so to speak, on my heart—but please try to give it no more thought at present . . . Furthermore, any attempt at explaining ourselves concerning that which we have suffered can only diminish the greatness of the conflict: *the conjunction of two extreme felicities*, that's its name—no heart could be large enough to contain them both simultaneously— and it is quite clear that I was wrong to put my only home to torch at the moment when I had been commanded to serve up that other fire, the one that does not consume! But even that judgment is not quite fair: *it is, I am sure, a greatness of pure destiny, that goes so far beyond us that we are not even allowed to take the blame within it. What happened to us, and to you too, Dearest, is neither petty nor degrading, but* too great. *If, therefore, there is any need of consolation, let it be that—everything else, what it might mean for me, you must let go; I can neither share nor speak of it—one day, no doubt, the notes which I wrote out my last week but one at Berg will convey certain things to you. The last thing, too, remains unsaid; God forbid it should ever be put into words—I couldn't bear it.*

For the moment, Beloved, I am only concerned with your health. Every morning that brings the promise of untold splendors, amongst so many blooming roses, I am deeply grieved not to be able to bring you out on the terrace here—how comfortable you would be in the sunshine; you would want for nothing, nothing, nothing . . . yesterday the terrace, though much smaller, reminded me of the one in Sierre. "Look" (I say to you, whom I felt so close), "look at the peonies in their red gowns, and the roses open wide" (they're losing their petals now), but the roses, the roses! My Beloved, I do not show you all this to make your yearning even more unbearable, but to see this youthful summer is to show it to you; I could not see it otherwise . . .

But from what I read in your letters, I can't help feeling that the time has come, above anything else, for you to take that cure—still, don't be discouraged if those first outings were painful; you will progress in leaps and bounds; you'll see, one day you'll be walking without even being able to recall that yesterday it was otherwise.

125

But where to take this cure? Of course, I am not of the opinion that you must choose between any of those hundreds of places where they boast of those most depressing and most German of mud baths, no doubt such as that Pomeranian "Lourdes," dismal thought, a Lourdes where there wasn't even a little shepherdess Bernadette—in which case, all that's really left are those awful crutches. Even Tolz in Bavaria, which you spoke of earlier, would be more acceptable.

And those Italian baths (in Monsumano, I believe, of which I heard a great deal from my friends, concerning a Countess R. who went there every year), they are very popular, and it's true that they are recommended above any other place of that kind; but if these baths, located in ancient caves, are excellent, I fear that their hygiene sometimes leaves something to be desired, and above all I do not have much confidence in Italian doctors, who are far behind the times for the most part. *Which you must not repeat,* at least not in such harsh wording, either to Mme. S. nor to her sister, since they are Italian.

As for Rippoldsau, it's like this: . . . Its advantages: it is one of the oldest baths in Germany, and retains the noble facilities of these old resorts. Marvelous avenues: *a group of old houses, and channelled medicinal springs enclosed under little pavilions; all this was perfectly noble in the oldest sections. It was once the property of the Furstenberg princes who, until but a few years ago, still kept on an old, greystone house there as a pied-à-terre. Later, it was acquired by a jovial Mr. G. whom I knew in his old age, and after him, by a corporation. Naturally, these two recent owners have* restored and ruined many things—which was inevitable in any case, especially since the entire resort, including its old trees, being situated at the very end of a gorge in the Black Forest mountains—near the Wurtemberg border—its ancient buildings were not without the mildewed smell of a cave. In remedy, they built the new hotel—certainly the most expensive, the so-called "Villa Sonnenberg" (pictured on the back of the brochure) about halfway up the southern slope of the mountain. This house offers every convenience you could hope for: the rooms are reminiscent of the Bellevue in Berne, they have a little private dining room there where, at tables carefully isolated one from another, you were served in deepest silence and with great discretion in my time, so much so that the lovely, unhappy Countess Merenberg (née Princess Jurievsky, granddaughter of Tsar Alexander), despite her suffering state, always appeared at table. It was the dining room for the hypersensitive, for those who wanted to avoid everyone. Proust could have described the way we were served by the waiter: he took us each to be so timid that he had a special way of presenting himself, before offering us the plate; a whole system of precautions preceded this gesture, from which no one, afterwards, could really claim to have suffered the slightest harm. But these are already old memories. I see that there is a new doctor, and it is likely that many things have since changed; before the war there were many Alsatians (Strasbourg is nearby), even some French, Russians, tout ce qu'on voulait. The mud baths are pleasant, the bathing facilities at "the height" of perfection—and staying at the Sonnenberg, one is not often obliged to go down (except for the baths) to the bathing holes, where naturally they have resort concerts and that sort of thing—but not a great deal of

"bustle." On every side one is surrounded by vast forests—mind you, few paths that aren't steep at the beginning.
　　And the Bohemian *resorts—shouldn't you also give them a thought, in the end? They are justly famous for their mud! The reasons keep mounting up that sooner or later I should go spend some time in Bohemia* . . . If the doctor decides that you must absolutely take your cure first, wouldn't it be advisable to begin it as soon as possible, that is, at the time when you must leave your brother's apartment? I dare not give you too much direction as to where to go, since, from experience, I am only familiar with Rippoldsau. You have to rely a little upon *instinct,* as for that matter I did in coming here, *which, for having been undertaken so blindly, was astonishingly, magically, the right thing to do—alas, alas, for myself alone! In any case, one can hardly say "it is magic," as one might say "it's raining," "it's snowing," and never in the* first person—that I could never dare to do!

René

Letter XXXV
Le Prieuré d'Étoy
Canton of Vaud
May 19, 1921

My dear, my tender, my beautiful Friend,

It seems hardly plausible that I have managed to write to you—you too, in your many letters, of which I received three this morning, you *speak* to me, the pen seems barely to serve any purpose in them—you speak to me, Beloved, and if you ask whether I hear your voice, I can assure you that, *yes*, I hear it—it is sweet and painful to my ears.

My poor Friend, what it's like for me, knowing that throughout your body and in the greater part of your heart you are suffering so—do you know what it's like for me? And if I admire you with J. I fear for you with G., if you are using morphine to sleep. My tender Friend, instead of that, place this letter over your eyes, that it may serve as their lids.

You have not shared my suffering, my Beloved; you

have gone through far worse in remaining day and night (how long?) under the tyranny of this atrocious illness. As for me, I have suffered greatly and suffer still, but what is making me suffer is a bad conscience which I cannot share with anyone and must bear alone! For the worst is not my having to leave Berg (I am used to leaving places dear to me, and this exercise of dying to an environment that has long sustained me will forever be a part of my heart's apprenticeship). My deepest torments come from my having been unable to give the form I would have wished to this past winter . . .

Those days, my God, they rushed by so quickly toward the end, and there were so many little roots to be withdrawn from that hospitable soil that I had almost no time to think about the future. A few days before my departure my attention was drawn to a very small advertisement placed in the *Journal de Genève.* I had just enough time to write for additional information—they were reassuring enough for me to have spent only one night in the Baur-au-Lac . . . The situation here is just as it was described in the classified ad—everything is fine, calm—I have a bright room that looks out on the lake in the distance, a flat panorama, broken by a solitary pop-lar, my bed is in an alcove at one end, and, what is quite lovely, a flowering rosebush climbs up to my window; already generously blown, the "Dijon Glories" perme-ate with their perfume this little corner where I remain locked up almost all the time, taking all my meals here. The garden is not big—a wide terrace that loses itself in a somewhat sickly orchard to the right. I don't go there often, so as not to mingle with the other boarders, from whom I hold myself completely aloof, having no great urge, you can understand, to make acquaintances.

But beyond this orchard, just guess, Beloved, guess what I can see: the tower of Aubonne Castle—it's only an hour and a half from here . . . If we had continued our stroll leading to that village, which doubtless you recall, within a half hour or so we would have reached Étoy!

Oh my Beloved, what memories!

Of course, my first idea was Sierre—but that would have been too expensive (I must make do with little during the rest of my stay in Switzerland), and then I didn't dare to go there without you . . . (Two months ago, I bought a few lottery tickets. Two drawings have since been held; it seems that fortune, absentminded as usual, is busy elsewhere!) No, you can imagine that I could not bear to go to Geneva—in a few days, if I feel a little rested, I'll mention to the Ss that I would like to see them before I go; perhaps they will be enterprising enough to come see me here . . . and then I am expecting Princess von Thurn und Taxis, whom I would so have wished to receive at Berg; toward the end of the month, she plans to go to Rolle to see her lovely grandchildren, who are at boarding school there.

I have long needed to see once more this revered friend who, through many years, advised me in all my plans . . . I would like to discuss with her this move to Bohemia that has been anticipated for so long; it is difficult to go over all the details by letter. The little house across from L. castle[1] that the prince tried to keep for me had to be given up under pressure from the municipality, but perhaps if I go there in person, some change in attitude can be effected in the authorities—I should like to discuss all this with the princess before making any firm plans . . . In any case, I'll need something along the lines of Berg for the autumn, not so as to begin the winter which will be on the way, but so as to *re*begin, with a stronger will, the winter divided between anxieties and happiness, far from that foundation of serene labor upon which I had hoped to erect it. I speak to you of this in all candor (how could I do otherwise), and I feel strong enough to banish from my feelings, often so deeply bitter, any shadow of reproach that might fall upon your bright and lovely countenance. It is to myself alone that I must account for my lack of firmness, and I would rather give up my life as I envision it than allow my ingratitude to rise against your heart, as wonderful as a rose and as generous as an entire, felicitous garden.

But where, my tender Friend, where are the great trees of *our* summer, which I saw nevertheless in the flash of a sublime clairvoyance? You speak of going to take a cure at Tölz . . . Certainly you will need, my Beloved, you will need above all a good treatment, a cure diligently followed. I would find it infinitely sweet, my Friend, to be at your side during this convalescence;

1. Lautschin, an estate belonging to the von Thurn und Taxis family, in Bohemia.

it seems to me that my solicitude could never be more beneficial to you than then, and that it alone is capable of erasing the memory (larger than nature) of such corporeal and heartfelt suffering.

In great draughts I am drinking of the ineffable satisfaction of being once more in French speaking territory, and I have yet to make any well-defined notion of the time when I shall have to cross the border hitherto avoided.

Communications with Gide continue. This morning I had a very nice letter from him; he has just shown Valéry the few lines from my last letter that could have been of interest to him. Arriving here, I found a book, also published by the Éditions de la Nouvelle Revue Française, that Jean Schlumberger had just dedicated to me; I was completely absorbed in reading its moving passages which in places attain the happy precision of a masterpiece. This parcel greatly helped me to bear the first moments in a strange environment, which offended me at first by the inevitable inconveniences of life in a *pension*, which I had just about forgotten.

And so I find myself, at the end of my Swiss sojourn, very near the vicinity where I began it, two years ago; the view from my window reminds me a good deal of the one I had from that "Farm" in Nyon where Countess D. used to have her guests when her little chalet couldn't fit them all. Unfortunately, she is still in England, whence she will go directly to Czechoslovakia.

Beloved, I must finish here! Ah, do not be fooled by the apparent calm affected in this letter—I am mastering myself; but no less than you, my poor Friend. I am longing to see you, to take your face, made thinner by so much suffering, between these two gentle hands, and never to tire of looking at it.

What to do, how to go about making you feel just a little bit of my tenderness? Read well between the lines, my Beloved, my Friend, my sweet child, rest, sleep, and smile a little at each attempt of happiness to awaken within you.

René

Letter XXXVI
June 6, 1921, Monday, toward night
Le Prieuré d' Étoy
Canton of Vaud

It is too tempting, my beloved Friend, to use your lovely gift of writing paper straight away—in exchange, I've sent you the *Vogue* (June edition) from Lausanne, where I spent a few hours.

The princess has yet to make herself known. "My venerable protectress"—as you call her a bit maliciously, for that is something she has never been. Have you not noticed, my Friend, that you always manage to speak with some irony, or even with an incomprehensible harshness, about those people who are dear to me through abiding friendship? It grieves me only because it makes it more or less impossible to speak to you of them, *arglos und einfach*,[1] as the mood takes me. I well

1. Innocently and simply.

know that it is your suffering expressing itself in this manner—it is not your own voice—but don't you think that we have much to gain by forcing our pain to sing only that which we are . . .?

I too, my tender Friend, could do many a wrong were I to allow my heart to avenge itself for all that it has been made to suffer for months; but I must confess that, on the contrary in my case, without boasting, I rejoice when you tell me about your friends and, even without knowing them, I grow to love them to the extent that I feel you loved by them. On several occasions I have wanted to ask whether you had tried to look up the Russian friends you made in 1914 but I resisted so as not to awaken vainly their memory in you and now you write me with such tender intimacy of the hours you spent with those refined creatures; I am delighted. What pleasure it would give me to see them with you one day; a while back, I too was steeped once again in the Russian atmosphere, receiving a moving letter from a young friend who was thought lost in the war. And imagine, he writes that, for a certain time in Russia, I too was said to have been killed.

I will show you his beautiful letter. Have you read Schikele's[2] writings on his journey through Alsace and in Paris (*chez Barbusse*)? It's very beautiful. I have that number of the *Rundschau*, because Regina Ullman[3] sent

2. René Schikele, 1883–1940. German expressionist writer of poetry, novels, and plays.

3. Swiss poet, friend of Rilke.

it to me along with another little work of hers, very curious in spots but inferior to the *Wirthshausschild*. It's funny what you tell me, that the little anecdote that I read in Bonsels' autobiography refers to Mme. S's sister ... *Eros und die Evangelien* is not a good book, though very engaging and sometimes even facinating. It loses a lot in comparison to the *Menschenwege* where, at heart, the two subjects are treated with far more subtlety and moderation. *In* Eros und die Evangelien, *he makes too much of everything, unbearably, through sheer intention and precision.* Providing these two contrasts, he piles up exaggerations on both sides, but unfortunately, the two "cases" he presents go without saying, so to speak. The strength of the poor dying little girl, her God out of danger, lies in her silence—and that other character, contrarily very active, avoids expression from the opposite extremes, and does not make much of a case. *While he's on the shoemaker, it's wonderful; he should have stopped there! (That is what Lou Andreas-Salomé wrote in her report—and I know I felt the same way when I read it.) At any rate, from these two aspects of Bonsels also appears that which is praiseworthy in different places, with all the magic of his best moments. How beautiful, how heart-wrenchingly beautiful are the words spoken by the foreigner, in the garden beneath the open window.*

Oh my Friend, *"in the garden," I said; the little pictures in the last letter do not show you that of the Prieuré, one can't tell how wide it is, nor see the two enormous terraces where the vineyard begins, just behind the little wall. If you could see, if you could see the roses. All of this is a complete waste,*

and believe me, Beloved, I'm getting nothing from it; *my
eyes take nothing in of all this before them—never but with
your own would mine dare to take possession. I know this
every day, and do not commit the least violation of joy, no
matter how close nor how willing to give of itself everything
might be. A few days of rain, many thunderstorms almost
immediately followed by an intrusive heat—and everything
gave way to an irresistible blooming, the jasmine shone with
its stars as when the Salises were here (now it's quite extinguished despite a few late blossoms), I saw laburnum somewhere, and a hail of acacias—is it conceivable that the
lindens will flower and we not breathe them together! Merline, I have had so many conversations with my destiny, day
and night, after which [a trip to] Muzzano seemed less clear
and plausible (perhaps because I don't know the area), but
Sierre, Sierre—I kept seeing us in Sierre: it seems to me that
destiny owes it to us to bring us there, on our terrace, with our
books* . . . Dearest, if one desires, if one believes, everything is possible; as soon as my guest has left, wouldn't
you like to join me? I have already written to the Hotel
Bellevue; I received a very nice reply—I don't think
there will be much of a crowd there at the moment. It
would also be lovely at the "Prieuré" for myself alone,
holding aloof, I'm not much aware of the boarders, nor
of the size—but with two of us we might feel how
cramped it is, and we would after all be very conspic-
uous in this restrained environment. And then, in the
Valais, we would have that wide open, that marvelous
countryside. I write you this, my dear Friend, because
this image keeps overwhelming me with its immense
promise . . . The lake, at certain spots along its shore,

reminds me of the landscape around Ville d'Avray, and of those lakes that Corot loved to paint; at times it has that tender and luminous atmosphere that I have known nowhere else in that heavy Bavaria, with its sky patriotically adorned with the colors of its flags . . .

R.

Grand Hotel Chateau Bellevue
Sierre Valais
Autumn, 1921

Dear Merline,

I am at the Bellevue, and before going up to our good
and faithful Muzot, which henceforth will be mine with
all the heart which you awoke in it, I hastily send you
this little greeting for your awakening in Zurich. Before
you leave again, let me read the results (if there are any)
of your negotiations in Berne, and keep your spirits up,
for there is more continuity in everything than you
believe! May God give you the confidence to *do right* and
to lose nothing of the riches that he lavished upon us to
the point of making us stagger beneath them.

Have a few more good days with those true friends
which the Strohl's[1] are, and do not be too sensibly upset

1. Jean Strohl, a zoology professor, and his wife Frida, were old
friends of Merline's husband Erich.

by the mournful border. Your wonderful visa is not merely an opportunity; it is a presage of better fortune to come.

I raise my eyes (I am at the little table, to the right as you enter the library) and I find that the campanula painted on the wall panel are fairly lightly done, and such that they react upon the memory: how much we partook of that happiness of being a part of summer, of being, for a moment, the consciousness of all summers.

I've already been to Jegerlehner's to see the writing stand, whose measurements I marked on my cane; it is really very pretty, and screwed onto a little table it should be strong enough to support me and all my meditation.[2]

The neglected fleece has fallen from my head, and I'm leaving now to make a good beginning. I shall forcibly borrow from everywhere—from all the memories and even from the great sadness that unites us today. Do as much yourself, Merline, do as much yourself.

René

2. Like many writers, Rilke always wrote standing up. Wherever he travelled, he had a new standing desk made to his own specifications.

Letter XXXVIII
Chateau de Muzot-Sur-Sierre
Valais
December 24 Christmas (the night itself)

Merline, Beloved,

Yet another parcel from you has just arrived, at 8:30 on Christmas Eve. I open it, my Friend, *what a noble surprise you have given me*—it is so beautiful, so gracious, so moving!

Thank you.

Do you know what I said after having admired *how you have "transformed" and enlivened and entirely filled with charm this figurative portrait?* I said, at last I have the parents I need.

At noon, though I have only just now opened it, your other parcel arrived from Geneva: merci; the Chasseriau, Sapho,[1]

---

1. Théodore Chasseriau, 1819–1856. French painter. The painting (1852) shows Sappho flinging herself from the rock of Leucades.

how beautiful. You can guess where it will go: in the window reveal, opposite your portrait. And then the third thing: practical and so very necessary; of such magnificent shell, strong and soft to the touch; I used it then and there.*

Thank you.

I am pleased to have had, also this evening, a nice letter from G. that speaks to me as I read it, it so captures his little voice.

Mme. W.[2] presented me with a candlestick just like the R.'s, but exactly, that sits on my little bookcase next to the door.

And a box for pens, tacks, etc., with a glass cover under which is a lovely (English) color print of *Sion,* the box itself is lined with her own paper.[3] And then, a marvelous gift: *a briefcase like the one of mine you took (did she know?) in the loveliest light grey chamois leather! A most generous thing.*

From the Salises, a mysterious flask sealed with their coat of arms, the contents of which I cannot imagine.

From Basel a splendid cyclamen, blooming red; a few books from here and there.

But the most astonishing thing, which fills my entire heart, is the drawing, your painting so inspired, so light,

---

* This comb was truly chosen by a connoisseur.

2. Nanny Wunderly, a devoted friend of Rilke and tireless supplier of material and emotional support.

3. Nanny Wunderly practiced bookbinding as a hobby.

so dreamy—it is truly miraculous that you could make such a thing. You must tell me *how* the idea came to you. I keep running in to look at it.

The Ponts (Villa Paradis, the innkeeper in Chandolin) invited Frieda[4] *to hear the midnight mass, so I shall be entirely alone in the silent house from 11:30 onward. It has been snowing since yesterday, but even more heavily since this morning. While I was downstairs eating my gruel around seven, there was suddenly a light from across at Saint Anne's [Chapel]. Frieda noticed it, and went over there while I was at the table; someone had lit two candles there and then gone. The door bolted. No one. Saint Anne alone with two candles!*

A good holy night, Beloved; you gave me the *greatest joy* that anyone could imagine.

Good night.

René

4. Frieda Baumgartner, Rilke's housekeeper.

Letter XXXIX
Thursday night
February 9, 1922

Merline, I am saved!

That which weighed upon and tortured me is accomplished, and, I believe, gloriously so. It took but a few days, but never within my heart and mind have I borne such a hurricane. I am still trembling from it—tonight I was afraid of collapsing; but no, I overcame ... And I went out to caress this old Muzot, just now, in the moonlight.

Now can begin the calm labor, well-balanced, quotidian, confident—which will seem *wie eine Windstille*,[1] after this divine tempest, too strong for anyone ...

I cannot write. But you will be satisfied with these

---

1. Like a lull in the wind.

good tidings. Send me yours, Beloved, Beloved—dear
Friend . . .

René

P.S. I am sending you the Valéry . . . copied out a
fortnight ago, but which I haven't had time to post.
You'll see how beautiful it is, how sublime—in places—
though perhaps not as ''far'' as *Eupalinos*[2]—furthermore, it seems that this dialogue takes place while they
are still on earth. In this alone, it cannot achieve the
ultimate independence of the other.

Your hyacinth has poked through the little islet of
soil, just think! After only four days!

2. *Eupalinos ou l'architecte* (not published until 1923).

Letter XL
Château de Muzot
Thursday, May 11, 1922

My Beloved Friend,

Happily, letters travel fast these days—I've just received yours of May 9—and I hasten to write you, dear, dear Merline; would that I could bring you a little, just a very little consolation, my very dear Friend . . . I too have had days that do not number amongst my best—spring has been here since May 5, but the sudden change (it turns hot from one moment to the next, that rich Valais heat you know so well) can affect one's health; one feels worn out beneath the insistent weight of the sun and after that long wait, instead of celebrating springtime, one tolerates it!

My beloved, fear nothing for yourself; I'm sure it's your nerves, overworked by this too protracted stay, that give you the annoying sensation of being "affected in the head, in the heart" ... I too, reacting to the tension of work, which was severe this time, often find myself at the mercy of various illnesses—which I resist, by the way, with a steadfast will! I had some visits: the Salises for Easter, later Mme. W. All the time he spent here, W.R.[1] was visibly suffering from having to make a decision; his discomfort was quite similar to the one in which you saw me during those days of uncertainty preceding our move to Muzot! And he had no one by his side to support him, as you did me imperturbably in our predicament back then, for I dared neither to advise the purchase to him, nor to discourage it. I wanted his final decision to *come from him alone, in no way influenced by my opinions or my desires.* And I understood perfectly his difficulty in reaching a satisfactory conclusion, all the more so since young Raunier,[2] before divesting himself of his manor, resisted all suggestion with such firm stubbornness that the Colonel,[3] who tried very hard to remain fair to both sides, began to lose patience. At times, his position was very difficult. Furthermore, W.R. left without making a decision, but imagine, along with your letter, this very day (might you have felt the neces-

1. Werner Reinhart, a Winterthur businessman and patron of the arts who would rent and eventually buy Muzot for Rilke.

2. The Raunier family owned Muzot. Mme. Raunier, the matriarch, had recently died, making the sale possible.

3. Colonel Souvairan, the Rauniers' guardian.

sity of being at Muzot for the occasion?) I received from W.R. the following good news: Muzot is his. He came to an agreement with the Colonel; he is now the purchaser, providing that no new, unforeseen difficulties should arise. One never knows with the Rauniers . . . Since Easter the brother has grown sick of clipping beards, which he does rarely enough anyway, since *two* are required in the exercise of that profession, and there were few men willing to allow him access to their beards . . . so one day he declared to poor Anni Raunier that he's had enough . . . Henceforth, he wants to be a photographer and sell photographic accessories. He began by going in with M. Zuf, the "artist"—you remember him—who runs the *Sierre* Cinema, and he has already had a pompous sign painted which one of these days will be hung above the shop, proclaiming in enormous letters: PHOTO-HALL.

That, Dearest, is what is happening here—it rarely brings a smile to my face, as smiling does not come easily to me. Our garden is making us a lot of work in watering, while giving little in return for the moment. Everything is terribly late. *One* red tulip has opened in the past week, in the border by the front door; the others are just beginning . . . those in the middle are still completely closed . . . I'll speak to you another time about the garden and myself, Beloved—I'd like Frieda to post this without delay; she's already getting ready to head down . . .

You moved me to the center of my heart by adding that photo of the rue Bara—oh my dear Merline, what can I say? I *know* I saw you that way and you know that I have never forgotten it . . . This one is the ancestor of all my later memories bearing your name, Merline, and it remains as ineffable as the others.

René

Letter XLI
Grand Hotel Château Bellevue
June 12, 1922

This is the first time in a while, Merline, that I recognize your writing from the good old days; even the envelope was like one of your watercolors—and as for the letter, it seemed to have covered in one wing beat the entire distance!

Merline, Beloved, you know how I've wished that you might be able, independently of our sufferings and the pains we have experienced, to feel as immanent and effectual the innumerable riches that from my heart have gone out to yours. If you have managed to do so, how sweet will be the day of our reunion, my dear friend.

If I never speak to you of *my* heart it is because I have not yet dared to examine it since it slipped from the hand of that God who shook it so strenuously during the months of work. I confess that I still feel as if I were convalescing from those creative emotions, and a bit like one who, with trembling knees, comes down again from the highest peak, from his elemental, unexplored, and ineffable nature . . .

Your letter before last, Beloved, so full of bitterness, so angry with me, threw me even deeper into that silence within myself. You had no curiosity about my guests—and here again, coincidentally, I find myself once more in the midst of a "series," but after the 15th or 20th of June there will remain only the K.'s (a visit of the greatest importance) to come, and, I hope, bring up the rear of this long processional of friendship.

In any case, you'll find me at the Bellevue for about another fortnight; I had long promised Frieda a few moments of vacation, for she had nothing left to wear against the heat, which here (as everywhere) is beating down full force. I'm not sure of being able to bear an entire summer in the Valais, without a little break from the heat somewhere. But I have no definite plans as yet.

And you, Dearest—please do not keep any more of your letters; send them all, especially those which might tell me something of your ideas for the summer . . .

Au revoir, Merline—write to

René

Letter XLII
Chateâu de Muzot-Sur-Sierre,
Valais, Hotel Bellevue
June 21, 1922

My dear Friend,

So you're coming to Switzerland! It's only right after
all, all these days, since the rose bower is beginning to
bloom—and you know how fast that happens here! I
cannot go up to Muzot without being reproached by the
garden for your absence; it is entirely turned toward
Merline—as for me, I am tolerated.

Beloved, you were born invited to Muzot; I'd tell you
to come here directly after crossing the border, if it
weren't your desire to be alone a while during your stay
with Francine, which certainly might have its attrac-
tions for a few weeks. But if it doesn't come off as you
had hoped, for one reason or another—Muzot is always
here, *always* awaits you, and God knows whether, here
too, you could find the desired solitude, for it sometimes
seems to me that I am quite tired of this country, and

that perhaps I need a change much greater than the Bellevue to be steeped once more in reality, which is blunted here (despite its magnificence) for having suffered too much and for having insisted too strongly on its own qualities and the intimate succor of its generous surroundings. But as I told you in my last letter, I hardly know myself, and I may be mistaken about the reasons for my quasi-indifference to the young summer that will delight your grateful eyes. Perhaps, too, I can adopt your way of seeing, if your joy is strong enough to uplift me as far as its point of departure (which will coincide exactly with that of its arrival).

Since my friends went home to Montreux, I have found myself almost alone at the hotel. It's delightful—I have the whole terrace to myself . . . the apricot trees, alas, will be unable this year to make us their generous morning offerings; they were the ones to be sacrificed to the last frost of this tardy spring—but the other trees in the orchards hold great promise, and the flowering vine begins the long, passionate simmering of its future clusters.

Do not think from what I stated above that I am ungrateful for this beautiful country, to which I am forever bound by so many memories; but I can't see it as well, either from passing fatigue, or from that involuntary laziness that envelops us when we think we "know" a place, forgetting that it is our admiration which might at any time turn things so as to make them seem new and inexhaustible. This time, my dear Merline, Muzot will have to return what you lent it of your strength, when you busied yourself with such warm and imperturbable conviction in setting up the household, its living existence . . . You will have rest, or if work, your own! Don't forget to bring all your painting materials; you will create the Art of the Valais, since you well know there's no one to do it. Again yesterday, toward the evening, strolling down a path which you don't know (I discovered it later) I called to you several times over, and I would have liked to set you straight away before the "motif" which so loved you . . .

What splendor, the shadows' softness, the purity of this landscape's "characteristics"—really, at certain moments it seems to possess all that makes up the charm and the spirit of a beloved face.

Really, who am I telling?

Do you remember the date of that first day we came up to Muzot with Mlle. Raunier? I didn't make a note of it, and I'm not even sure I remember the date when we first moved into Muzot . . . Will you be here for one of its anniversaries? No, we should rather celebrate that of the wonderful Sunday morning when we stood on the slope across from Muzot, without being yet able to go in . . . you busied yourself sweetly with the first "portrait" of Muzot and I, in the meantime, went to kneel in the little white chapel . . . Do you remember how long and fine that morning was, and light and all infused with tender blessings? Try, if you can, to recall the date . . .

René